A to Z 神秘案件

中英双语
第一辑

The Invisible Island

隐形岛

[美] 罗恩·罗伊 著
[美] 约翰·史蒂文·格尼 绘 高琼 译

湖南少年儿童出版社
HUNAN JUVENILE & CHILDREN'S PUBLISHING HOUSE
小博集 BOOKY KIDS
·长沙·

人物介绍

三人小组的成员，聪明勇敢，喜欢读推理小说，紧急关头总能保持头脑冷静。喜欢在做事之前好好思考！

丁丁

三人小组的成员，活泼机智，喜欢吃好吃的食物，常常有意想不到的点子。

乔希

三人小组的成员，活泼开朗，喜欢从头到脚穿同一种颜色的衣服，总是那个能找到大部分线索的人。

露丝

罗恩·平科夫斯基

罗恩鱼饵店的店长，也帮助别人保养船，为人热心。因为曾经在药店买过炉甘石药膏，被三人组怀疑是在少女岛藏假钞的嫌疑人。

沃登·本特

刚搬来绿地镇的居民，经常开着一辆时髦的林肯汽车。被三人组怀疑是在少女岛藏假钞的嫌疑人。

本特太太

刚搬来绿地镇的居民，养了一条短腿猎犬。因为这条猎犬，三人组在调查案件的时候差点被发现。

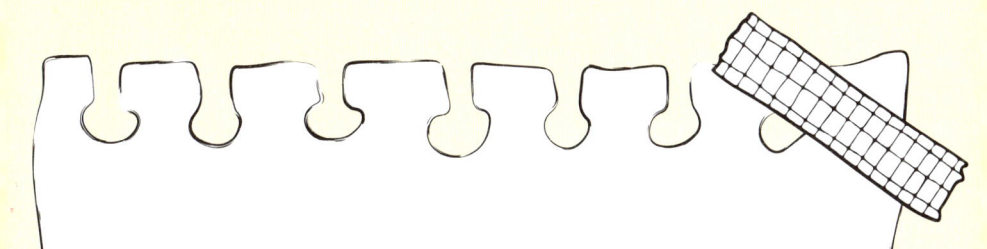

字母 I 代表 illusion，幻觉……

一沓又一沓的绿色钞票成摞地堆在一起。丁丁放眼望去，看到的全是一摞一摞的钱。

"这里面肯定有好几百万美元！"乔希一边说，一边闭上了眼睛，"我觉得我快要吐了。"

…………

突然，丁丁扭头向后面看去。"嘘！"他小声地说，"我想我听到了什么声响！"

…………

雾气中传来一声低沉的"吱呀"声。接着是一片寂静，随后又是"吱呀"一声。

丁丁大口大口地喘着气，僵在了那里。"声音越来越近了！"他小声地说。

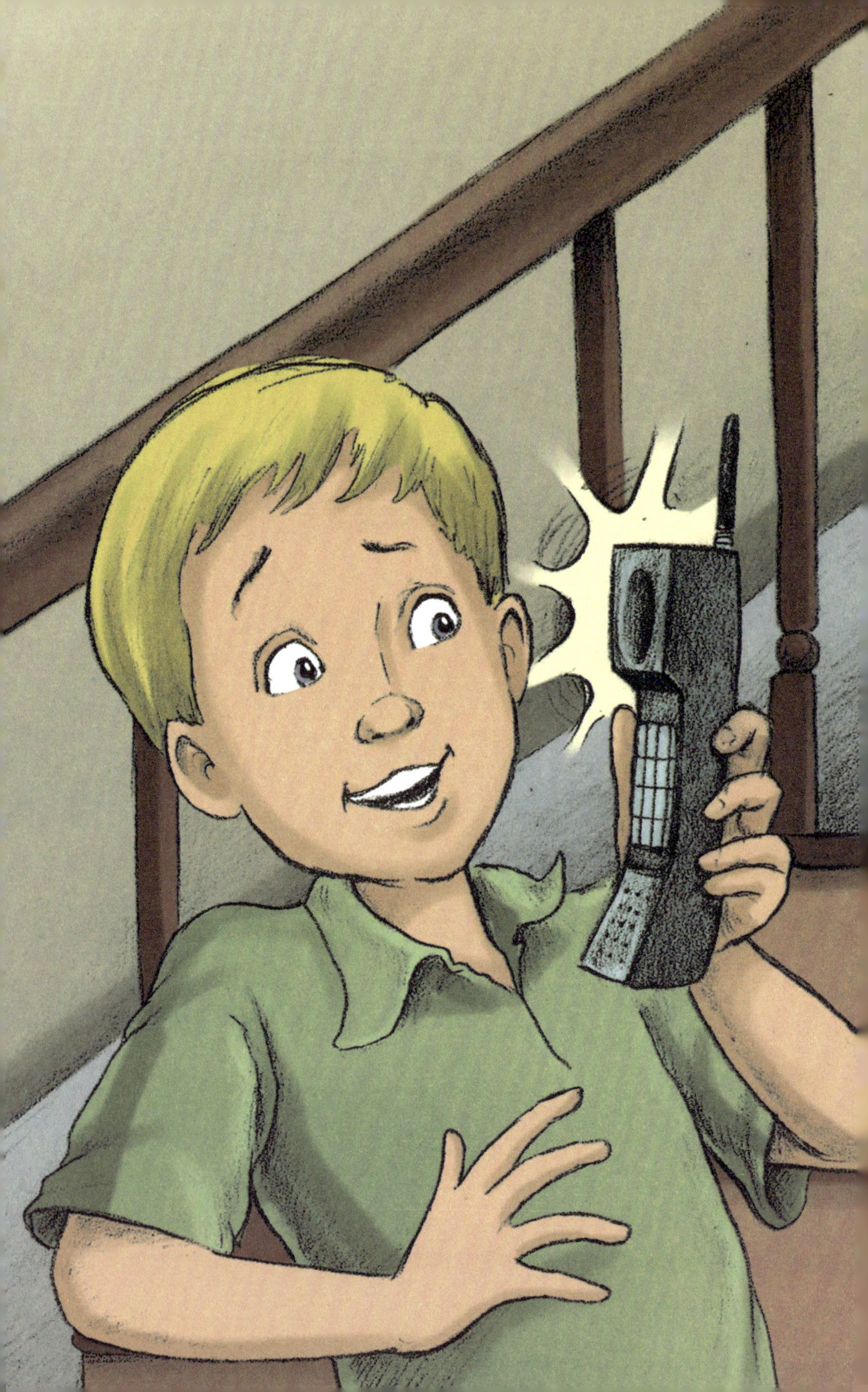

第一章

唐纳德·戴维·邓肯，朋友们都叫他丁丁，正在接电话。

"这是邓肯家，我是丁丁。"

"快过来！"乔希·平托大喊。

丁丁猛地把电话从耳朵边拿开。"怎么啦？"他问道。

"我妈妈说咱们可以去少女岛野餐，"乔希

说,"她还给咱们做了午餐!"

现在是七月,热浪蒸腾。在印第安河里嬉戏玩耍一定很爽,丁丁心里这样想着。

"好啊,我去告诉我妈妈一声,顺便把露丝叫上。我们马上就过来。"

丁丁跑到楼上他爸爸妈妈的卧室。他妈妈正坐在缝纫机前缝补丁丁的一条牛仔裤。

"嘿,妈妈,我、乔希和露丝打算去河边野餐,可以吗?"丁丁问道。

"去吧,不过你们几个要待在一起,不要走散了。"他妈妈说。

"谢谢妈妈!"丁丁一边说,一边套上那条旧短裤,穿上那双脏兮兮的运动鞋。离开之前,他喂饱了洛蕾塔,也就是他养的豚鼠。丁丁往楼下跑的时候听见它开心地吱吱叫着。

丁丁急匆匆地来到露丝家。露丝的猫咪——泰格,正在门前的台阶上给小猫咪喂奶。丁丁小心翼翼地绕开它们,按响了门铃。

门开了。露丝的小弟弟纳特站在门口。他两只手里各拿着一块饼干,嘴巴里还有一块。

"嘿，纳特。"丁丁跟他打招呼，"你姐姐在家吗？"

"她……呜……去……"纳特嘴里咬着饼干，含糊不清地说。

丁丁对着纳特眨巴着眼睛："你说什么呢？"

这时，露丝从纳特身边突然出现。"嘿，丁丁，有什么事吗？"她问道。

露丝·罗斯·哈撒韦喜欢全身上下穿同一种颜色的衣服。今天，她穿着蓝色T恤衫、蓝色短裤，还有蓝色运动鞋。此外，她那富有弹性的黑色卷发上还系着一条蓝色束发带。

"乔希想去少女岛野餐。"丁丁说。

露丝咧着嘴笑了。"太好了！"她转过身，向屋子里探去。"再见，妈妈！我要和我的两个朋友去野餐啦。"

她随即弯下腰，把小弟弟嘴巴上的饼干屑抹掉。"纳特，跟妈妈待在家里，好吗？我回来时给你带一块魔法石！"

纳特一边咧着嘴笑，一边跑回家里去了。

露丝把门拉上。随即，她和丁丁抄近路穿过

她家后院,然后横穿过老鹰巷。几分钟过后,他们就来到了乔希家。

此刻,乔希正在他家前院,手里拿着一根浇花的软管。他的两个弟弟——布赖恩和布拉德利正在水花里大声尖叫着,奔跑着。

"嘿!"看到丁丁和露丝,乔希一边打着招呼,一边把水管关了。

"我要走喽!"他对布赖恩和布拉德利说,"你们两个乖乖的,不要离开院子!"

乔希从门廊上一把抓起他的双肩背包。"希望你们俩肚子饿了。"他说,"我妈妈打包了很多吃的东西。"

"这些东西估计只够你吃三分钟!"丁丁一边说,一边咧着嘴笑。

孩子们徒步穿过乔希家后面的田野。随后,他们穿过沿河路,来到印第安河岸边。

河水缓缓地流淌着,在流经几块大石头时泛起了涟漪。大多数地方,河水很浅,孩子们可以蹚水而过。两侧河岸上长着乔木和灌木。小鸟和松鼠在郁郁葱葱的树林中叽叽喳喳地叫着。

隐形岛

孩子们沿着河流往前走，一路拍打着蚊虫。看见少女岛后，他们停下了脚步。

小岛坐落在河流中央。岛上满是沙子、灌木和石头。没有大树在这里生长，也没有动物在小岛上安家。不过，孩子们喜欢这里的沙滩，喜欢这里清澈、低浅的河水。

他们穿着运动鞋蹚进水中。很快，河水便漫到了他们的膝盖处。

"好家伙，这也太舒服了吧！"当凉丝丝的河水漫过他汗涔涔的双腿时，丁丁忍不住兴奋地叫起来，并用脚朝着乔希和露丝踢起水来。他们两个也哗啦啦地朝着他泼水还击。很快，三个人都湿透了。

几分钟过后，他们重重地坐到少女岛的小沙滩上。丁丁脱掉运动鞋，脚趾在温热的沙子上扭动着。

"咱们吃东西吧！"乔希一边说，一边打开自己的双肩背包，掏出来几个塑料袋。塑料袋里面装着三明治、切成块的西瓜，还有饼干。

"我在想，要是被困在小岛上会怎么样。"乔希说。

丁丁嘴里嚼着三明治。"乔希，咱们不会被困在这里的。咱们只要蹚过河水就能回到对面的河岸上。"

乔希两只眼睛望着远处。"说得没错。不过假如海盗在这里藏了宝物呢？"他一边说，一边用脚后跟在沙地上蹬出了一个坑。"我们屁股下面很可能就埋着一个装满黄金的箱子哟！"

"我觉得康涅狄格州根本就没有什么海盗。"露丝说。

"为什么没有啊？"乔希一边反问道，一边指了指小岛中央爬满藤蔓的大石头，"这里可是海盗藏身的绝佳之地！"

"好了，两位！"丁丁突然叫了一声。

露丝站起身来。"我想去探险。"她一边说，一边朝水中走去，"我答应过纳特，会给他带回去一块魔法石。"

"魔法石是什么东西啊？"丁丁好奇地问，然后跟在她后面来到水边。

"这个就是啊！"露丝拿起一块表面光滑、呈纯白色的鹅卵石。

"它会什么魔法?"

"纳特在自己的房间里放了一堆这样的鹅卵石。"露丝说,"我爸爸妈妈告诉他,如果他能保持房间整洁,这些石头就会变成五美分的硬币!"

这时,乔希也凑到了丁丁和露丝身边。他递给他们每个人一块饼干。"纳特真的相信吗?"他问道。

露丝咧着嘴笑了。"每次纳特打扫完房间,我妈妈就偷偷溜进去拿走一块石头!并在原来放石头的地方放上一枚五美分的硬币。"

孩子们开始沿着河岸往前走。阳光照在丁丁的背上,丁丁感觉很热,就把T恤衫脱了下来。

"嘿,两位,快看!"乔希大声喊道。只见他站在一个脚印上,说:"已经有人来过这儿了!"

他笑着对丁丁和露丝说:"说不定是黑胡子[1]呢!"

---

1. 黑胡子真名为爱德华·蒂奇,生于英国布里斯托尔,世界航海史上最臭名昭著的海盗之一。——译者

丁丁把自己的脚踩在这个脚印上。这个脚印有他的两只脚那么大呢!

"我没听说过黑胡子。"他说,"不过,不管他是谁,他的脚真大啊!"

"瞧,这儿还有一个脚印!"露丝说,"那边还有一个!"

孩子们顺着脚印往前走。脚印离水边越来越远,一路引导着他们来到了小岛中央的巨石堆。

在一块低矮扁平、爬满藤蔓的大石头前,脚印突然消失不见了。

"真奇怪。"丁丁说,"这个家伙去哪儿了,是从这些石头上跳过去了吗?"

"说不定他是从边上绕过去的。"乔希说。

丁丁和乔希开始绕着这些巨石慢慢地走,寻找更多的脚印。

露丝则朝着反方向寻找。突然,丁丁听见她大声地叫喊:"嘿,两位!快过来这边!"

丁丁和乔希转身往回跑去。

"瞧!"露丝一边说,一边指着她两只脚中间的地面。一个绿色的东西从沙地中露了出来。

"这是什么?"乔希迫不及待地问道。

"钱!"露丝大声回答道。

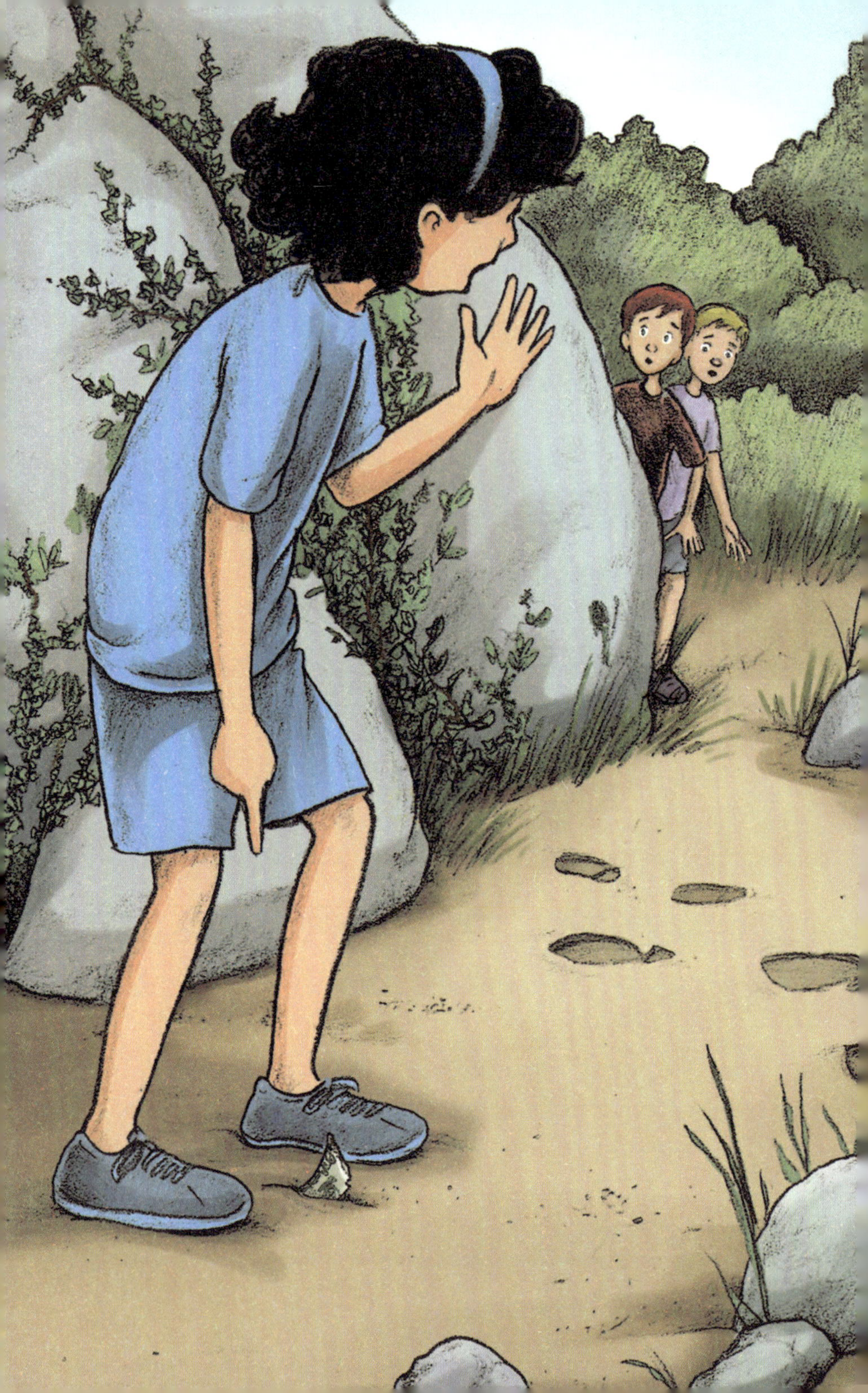

第二章

"是一张十美元的钞票呢!"乔希说着,一把抓起钞票,把它举了起来。

"不对,"丁丁一边说,一边从乔希的手上夺过那张钞票,"数数后面几个零吧!"

乔希惊讶得张大了嘴巴。

露丝那双蓝眼睛也睁得大大的。

丁丁手里正举着一张一百美元的钞票!

"一百美元啊!"乔希尖叫起来,伸手去拿钞票。不过丁丁迅速地把钞票还给了露丝。

"钱是她发现的。"他解释道。

"可是，钱是谁丢的呢？"露丝一边问，一边把钞票塞进了口袋。

丁丁指着沙地上的脚印。"说不定是这个人丢的。"

孩子们全神贯注地盯着这些脚印。

"说不定他丢的钱还不止这一张呢。"乔希说，"咱们再找找吧！"

于是，孩子们分头行动起来。他们爬过巨石，向灌木丛中窥探。他们一直盯着地面，发现了很多毒葛，但没有再找到百元大钞。

"嘿，你们两位，快看这个。"丁丁站在水边喊道。

乔希和露丝朝着丁丁站立的地方跑去。

丁丁指着一片长长的沙地。沙地表面非常光滑，看上去好像有人用木板在沙地上刮过，把所有不平整的地方都刮平了。

"我敢打赌，一定有人划船来过这里。"露丝说，"他们一定是从这里把船拖上沙滩的。"

"我在想，划船来到这里的那个人是不是就是留下脚印的那个人呢？"丁丁一边说，一边把

T恤衫重新穿上。

"还有,他是否就是掉了百元大钞的那个人。"乔希接过丁丁的话说。

露丝拍拍自己的口袋。"我不知道,不过咱们一定要想办法找到他。"

"为什么啊?"乔希一边说,一边咧着嘴笑,"想一想,咱们可以用这笔钱买多少东西啊。当然是咱们仨平分啦!"

"别惦记了,乔希。"露丝回答道,"这钱不是我们的。我们必须还回去。"

"问题是,还给谁啊?"

"谁丢的就还给谁。"丁丁说。

"那咱们要怎么样才能找到这个人?"乔希继续问道。

孩子们坐在沙地上思索起来。

"我想起来了。"露丝说,"咱们可以去罗恩鱼饵店问问。说不定平先生[1]知道谁来过这里。"

"好主意。"丁丁说。

---

1. 平先生即下文的罗恩·平科夫斯基。——编者

"哎哟。"乔希说着,站起身来,"你们两位这么想尽快把这笔钱还回去吗?"

"如果换作是你丢了张百元大钞,你会是什么心情?"露丝这样反问乔希。

乔希咧着嘴笑了:"放心吧,如果我真的有张百元大钞,我无论如何都不会把它弄丢的!别管它啦,咱们还是把我妈妈打包的西瓜吃掉吧。刚才吃了饼干,我已经口干舌燥了。"

孩子们回到乔希放背包的地方,津津有味地吃着一块块香甜多汁的西瓜。随即,他们一边收拾行李,一边互相吐西瓜子玩。

乔希耸了耸肩,把双肩背包背好。"好吧,如果我们必须归还这笔钱,说不定我们的名字会上报纸呢。"他一边说,一边挠了挠脚踝,"说不定我们会得到一笔赏金哟!"

露丝咯咯地笑起来:"乔希,你唯一能得到的是被毒葛划伤。"

第三章

孩子们再次蹚水往回走。几分钟过后,他们顺着沿河路往罗恩鱼饵店走去。

罗恩·平科夫斯基就住在河边的一栋老房子里。他在房子的第一层售卖鱼饵、船具和食品杂货。他也帮人修船,给船刷漆,还会给船安装发动机。

孩子们拖着沉重的脚步,沿着一条尘土飞扬的土路,艰难地来到了罗恩先生家。罗恩先生家的大院子紧邻河岸,好几艘小船在院子里排成一排。一只花斑猫躺在后门的台阶上睡觉。后门

处有一根长长的橙色绳子,孩子们顺着绳子绕到房子的一侧。

他们发现罗恩先生正在树荫下打磨一条船的船底呢。

"嘿,平先生。"丁丁打招呼。

这时,罗恩·平科夫斯基关掉了电动打磨机。他个子高高的,头发呈灰白色,脸上的胡子尤其引人注目。

"嘿,孩子们。你们今天来这儿有什么事吗?"他问道,脸上笑盈盈的。

露丝把那张百元大钞从口袋里掏了出来。"我刚刚在少女岛发现了这个。"她说。

"哎呀,"罗恩说,"你真是个幸运的姑娘!"

"我们在沙滩上看见了小船留下的痕迹。"丁丁说。

"还有一些脚印。"乔希补充道,"好大好大的脚印!"

"我们在想,这笔钱说不定是到过那里的人丢掉的。"露丝说。

A to Z 神秘案件

"嗯,我很好奇谁去过那儿。"罗恩斜靠在小船上,捋了捋自己的胡子,"去过那儿的人不多。那片沙滩上的毒葛特别厉害。"

"没错,我想我刚才正好踩到了毒葛丛!"乔希一边说,一边在一条腿上抓挠着。

罗恩笑了笑。"我只要看一眼那种东西,就会肿得像个气球。"他说。

"我们可以在您这儿留张字条说捡到了这笔钱吗?"露丝问道。

"主意不错啊,露丝。我会把它贴在我的鱼饵罐旁边的。"

孩子们跟着罗恩走进他的鱼饵店。他递给露丝一支铅笔和一本便笺簿。

露丝思忖了一会儿,动笔写道:

如果您在少女岛丢了钱,
请拨打电话 555-9916。

"你不是应该把捡到的钱的具体数额写上吗?"乔希问道。

露丝摇了摇头。"如果我写了具体数额,谁都可以打电话来认领,即便他们并没有丢钱。"

罗恩把露丝的字条用图钉固定在一块小小的告示牌上。"字条钉在这里会有很多人看到的。"他说。

"谢谢您,平先生。"露丝说,"真希望丢钱的人能看到这张字条啊。"

罗恩咧着嘴笑了,说:"真希望这个人就是我自己啊!"

孩子们哈哈大笑起来。随后,他们告别了罗恩,朝鸭子步行道走去。

"你打算怎么处理这笔钱?"乔希问露丝,"我很乐意替你保管哟!"

露丝摇了摇头。"不用。我要把它交给法伦警官。钱放在警察局最安全。"

乔希挠了挠自己的一条胳膊,说:"咱们半路上到埃莉餐馆一下吧。说不定吃个冰激凌甜筒之后,我就会忘掉这烦人的毒葛!"

孩子们穿过小学宽敞的草坪,沿着主街继续往前走。他们打开埃莉餐馆的门,一股冷空气扑面而来。

点完冰激凌甜筒之后,露丝问埃莉知不知道有人在少女岛丢钱了。

"那个人的脚真的好大哟!"丁丁补充道。

埃莉摇了摇头。"宝贝,我连谁去过那里都不知道呢。听说那里到处都是毒葛。"

她注意到乔希正在身上到处抓挠:"看样子某人也被那种东西划伤了!"

孩子们谢过埃莉之后离开了餐馆。他们一路吃着冰激凌甜筒,最后来到了警察局。

"真不敢相信我们就这么送出去一百美元。"乔希说。

"如果我得了赏金,"露丝说,"我会分给你们的。"

乔希咧着嘴笑了。"这还差不多!"

他们看到法伦警官坐在办公桌前,一边盯着电脑屏幕,一边小口地喝着玻璃杯里的柠檬汁。

孩子们排着队走了进去。"你们好,有什么

事情需要我帮忙吗?"法伦警官跟他们打招呼。

"看看这个!"露丝一边说,一边把那张百元大钞放到他的办公桌上。

法伦警官拿起钞票仔细看了看。"这钱是从哪里来的呢?"他问道。

"露丝在少女岛发现的。"乔希告诉他,"我们去那儿野餐,钞票就在沙地里!"

"我们正在想办法找丢钱的人呢。"露丝说,"罗恩先生让我在他的告示牌上钉了一张字条。我把我的电话号码留下了。"

"这张钞票可能丢失在那里很长时间了。"法伦警官说,"去少女岛的人不多。"

他朝露丝咧着嘴笑了。"如果没有人来认领,这笔钱就归你了。"

"真的吗?"露丝说,"太酷了!"

法伦警官把钞票装进一个信封并密封好。随后,他在信封外面写上日期和露丝的名字。

"我会把这个放进我们的保险箱。"他说,"如果过了三十天钱还在这儿,无人认领,我会通知你的。"

A to Z 神秘案件

孩子们谢过法伦警官后就离开了。

"天哪,露丝。"他们在主街等红绿灯的时候,乔希说,"如果这一百美元留给你,你会分成三份吗?"

"很可能会哟。"她说,"前提是你能对我格外好!"

"我一直都对你很好啊!"

突然,丁丁对着露丝的一只耳朵小声地说着什么。

隐形岛

"好吧,为了证明你对我很好,"她对乔希说,"明天去我家帮我修剪草坪吧!"

乔希哈哈大笑起来。"我有个更好的主意。咱们回到小岛上,去找找有没有更多的钱!"

"乔希,我们已经找过了,没有再找到钱。"丁丁说。

"可是我们一直都没有找到脚印的尽头。"乔希争辩道,"我敢打赌,如果我们找到了脚印的尽头,就能找到藏起来的宝藏!"

"那被毒葛划伤怎么办?"露丝提醒他。

乔希挠了挠他的脖子。"一点点毒葛算什么!"他说,"我打算明天再去一趟少女岛,而且我还要带上一把铁锹!"

他冲着两个朋友咧嘴笑了。"你们要跟我一起去吗?还是要我把宝藏全都留给我自己?"

第四章

第二天早上,丁丁打着哈欠,朝厨房的窗户外面望去。

"雾真大啊。"他嘟囔着。他喝完了燕麦粥,把碗放进水槽里。

就在这时,门铃响了。乔希拿着一把铁锹站在门廊上。"准备好出发了吗?"他问丁丁。

"雾太大了。"丁丁说着,往乔希身后望去,"我几乎都看不清街对面!咱们连小岛都找不到,更不要说宝藏了。"

"如果那里还有钱,我一定能找到的。"乔希一边说,一边挠了挠自己的脚踝,"咱们去叫露丝吧。"

"我已经来了!"露丝应声出现在大雾中。

看见乔希还在挠,她说:"你最好在被毒葛划伤的地方涂点药,乔希!"

"我妈妈也是这样跟我说的。"乔希一边说,一边在一条胳膊上挠了挠,"她让我去买点炉甘石药膏。咱们现在出发吧!"

乔希把铁锹扛在肩上,领着两个朋友穿过露丝家的后院,穿过牧场路。牧场路另一侧长着高高的野草,野草上的露珠把他们的运动鞋和双腿都打湿了。

靠近河边的地方,雾更浓了,像一小团一小团的云一样挂在树枝上。孩子们的脸和头发都湿了。

"我连河在哪儿都看不见。"丁丁嘟囔着。

"就在这儿啊。"乔希说着,用铁锹拍打着河里的水。

"好吧,可是小岛在哪儿呢?"露丝问道。

孩子们凝视着他们觉得应该是少女岛的地方。结果,他们只能看到弥漫着的大雾。只有一小块地方的雾看起来比其他地方颜色更暗一些。

"小岛肯定就在那里。"乔希一边说,一边走进水中,"快点,两位,我几乎已经闻到钱的味道了!"

"像猎犬鼻子一样灵。"丁丁小声地说。

河边静悄悄的,听不见鸟叫声,只能听见孩子们的腿在水中溅起水花的声音。

丁丁开始想象有只雾怪朝他爬过来。雾怪长着黏糊糊的绿色触须和六英寸[1]长的牙齿!

丁丁心里感到很庆幸——河水开始变浅了。突然,他的一只脚触碰到了干燥的陆地。他们又来到了少女岛上。

孩子们停下脚步四处张望着。缕缕雾气把一切都笼罩起来了。丁丁几乎分辨不出小岛中央的那堆巨石。他回想起昨天晒在背上的暖洋洋的太阳,不禁打了个寒战。

"这个地方在雾中令人毛骨悚然。"露丝说,

1.英美制长度单位。1英寸=0.0254米。——编者

"真希望太阳快点出来啊!"

"好吧,乔希。"丁丁说,"是你让我们来这儿的。现在该怎么办?"

乔希双手双膝着地,趴在地上。"帮我再找找那些大脚印吧。"他说。

孩子们迅速找到了那些大脚印,并顺着脚印来到那块低矮扁平、爬满藤蔓的巨石前。

"这双大脚的主人要从这里往哪儿去呢?"乔希喃喃自语道。

"看起来这家伙直接钻进了这块大石头里。"丁丁说。

"说不定他翻过了大石头。"露丝说。

乔希用铁锹杵了一下覆盖在大石头上的毒葛藤蔓。铁锹与石头相撞,发出丁零当啷的声音。乔希换了个地方又杵了杵。而这一次,铁锹直接插了进去。

"嘿,两位!"乔希说,"我想我发现了什么秘密!"

乔希用铁锹把藤蔓往后面拨,两只眼睛凝视着那个黑洞洞的地方。

"这里面有两块大石头!"他说。

"快看。"露丝说,"这两块石头中间有一条小路!"

小路十分隐蔽,上面爬满了毒葛的叶子和藤蔓。

"那个人肯定是从这里走过的。"丁丁说。

"可是这里到处都是毒葛!"露丝说。

"等一等。"乔希说。他用铁锹铲开毒葛,最后清理出一条通道。"咱们要小心点。"他说。

孩子们排成一列,一个跟着一个沿着狭窄的小路走去。一块块巨石耸立在孩子们左右两边。

不一会儿,他们来到一小块平坦的沙地上。沙地被石头环绕着,石头上爬满了毒葛。沾满露水的毒葛叶片在雾气中呈现出暗绿色。

"我感觉自己是在丛林中!"露丝说。

"又有脚印!"乔希一边说,一边双膝着地趴了下来。

丁丁也在乔希旁边趴下来。"这些脚印看上去像是同一个人留下的。"丁丁说,"可是这里的脚印太多了!而且,脚印跟脚印重叠起来了。"

"现在怎么办啊,乔希?"露丝问道。

"现在咱们寻找宝藏啊。"乔希说,"咱们轮流干,把这个地方全都挖一遍吧!"

于是,孩子们开始在沙地上挖坑,挖了一个又一个。露丝发现了一颗生锈的钉子,但没有发现任何宝藏。

很快,孩子们就累得汗流浃背,浑身沾满了沙子。乔希开始把沙子填回坑里,这样就不会有人踩进去了。

丁丁重重地坐在一块巨石上。

"当心!"露丝大声喊道。

丁丁从石头上跳了起来。有什么东西透过他的T恤衫刺痛了他!

"哎哟!是什么东西扎到我了?"他一边问,一边转过身,让乔希和露丝看看自己的后背,"你们看到什么了吗?"

乔希咧着嘴笑。"一大团毒葛而已。"他说。

"别笑了,快帮我弄下来!"丁丁大声叫道。

"我来帮你吧。"露丝一边说,一边用铁锹把那根毒葛藤条拨到一边。

"弄掉了吗?"丁丁一边问,一边努力扭头往后背上看。

"真是太奇怪了!"露丝说,"快看,乔希!"

"简直不敢相信啊。"乔希说。

"什么东西太奇怪了?"丁丁大声喊道,"你们两个在后面干什么呢?"这个时候,他已经感觉到身上发痒了。

"这根毒葛是假的!"露丝说。

"啊?"丁丁转过身来。露丝递给他一根带绿叶的树枝。树枝上的叶子是用塑料做的,枝条是用铜丝做的。

"我不明白。"丁丁说,"为什么有人……"

"太奇怪了。"乔希一边说,一边把铁锹头伸到覆盖在巨石上的假毒葛下面。随即,他扭动着铁锹,弄断了一截藤蔓。藤蔓从巨石表面整片地脱落下来,直挺挺地掉在地上。

"整块巨石上都覆盖着塑料做的毒葛呢。"露丝说,"假毒葛被系在了一个木架子上!"

"别管它了。"乔希说,"看看巨石下面是什么东西吧!"

这块所谓的"巨石"根本就不是巨石。面对眼前这个巨大的方形水泥箱,孩子们目不转睛地盯着,惊讶极了。

第五章

"这是什么?"丁丁和露丝异口同声地问道。

"看上去像一台水泥冰箱!"乔希答。

露丝哈哈大笑起来。"哇,乔希,我在想里面是不是装着吃的东西呢!"

"真好玩!"乔希爬上几块小一点的石头,然后爬到了水泥箱顶端。

"这上面也是平的。"他说,"这个东西是一个水泥做的大箱子!"

"这是门的正面吗?"露丝一边问,一边用铁锹杵了杵平坦的水泥板。

丁丁用手指摸了摸水泥箱的两侧。"找不到

合页啊。"他一边说，一边拽了拽水泥板，但水泥板丝毫没有动弹。

"说不定哪个地方装有暗锁呢。"露丝提示道。她开始绕着水泥板底部挖起来，但挖到的只有石头和毒葛根。

"哎哟！"乔希大叫一声，此时的他还待在水泥箱的顶部，"这上面有什么尖锐的东西呢！"

他从上面探出头来，叫道："爬上来吧，两位。我想我找到了打开这个东西的钥匙！"

于是丁丁和露丝爬到了乔希的身边。

"看看这个。"乔希一边说，一边指着水泥箱上凸出来的一根小小的金属棒。

"试着拉一下吧。"丁丁提议道。

乔希抓住金属棒，猛地一拉。

"拉不出来啊。"他嘟囔着。

"金属棒前后松动了吗？"露丝问道。

她用脚顶着金属棒，猛地一推。金属棒还是纹丝不动。

"好吧，得动真格了。"丁丁说。

于是他从水泥箱上爬下来，一把抓起铁锹，

递给上面的乔希。

"试试用这把铁锹砸砸看吧。"他说。

乔希把铁锹举过头顶,铆足了劲,用力朝金属棒砸过去。

突然,他们听到一阵刺耳的刮擦声,恰如人的指甲划过黑板发出的声音。

"哇,成功了!"丁丁一边大叫,一边往后跳,"它动了!"

水泥门自动打开了,一个潮湿、发霉的贮藏室露了出来。

丁丁向前走了一步,然后停下脚步。他嘴巴张得大大的。

隐形岛

"里面是什么东西啊?"乔希一边问,一边注视着下面的丁丁。

丁丁没有回答。

"丁丁?"露丝喊了一声,"出什么事了?"

丁丁大口大口地喘着气,努力想要开口说话。"气——气——气——"

"气气气,气什么啊?"乔希迫不及待地问道,"汽车?气球?还是气死我啊?"

此刻的丁丁几乎无法呼吸,更别提说话了。

"钱!"最后他总算把话说出来了。

第六章

乔希和露丝爬了下来,从水泥箱的开口往里面瞧。

里面就像银行的一个金库。金属架子用粗大的螺栓固定在水泥墙上。每个架子上都放着钱。

一沓又一沓的绿色钞票成摞地堆在一起。丁丁放眼望去,看到的全是一摞一摞的钱。

"这里面肯定有好几百万美元!"乔希一边说,一边闭上了眼睛,"我觉得我快要吐了。"

"不过,这是谁的钱呢?"露丝问道,"是谁把钱放在这里的呢?"

丁丁一脚踏进金库。最下面的架子上放着几

个纸板箱,纸板箱的侧面写着"开心狗粮"四个大字。

"是狗粮吗?"他说。

乔希和露丝也挤进了金库。露丝朝其中两个纸板箱里看了看。

"还是钱。"她说。

突然,丁丁扭头向后面看去。"嘘!"他小声地说,"我想我听到了什么声响!"

孩子们静静地站着,一动不动,仔细地倾听着。

"又听见了!"丁丁说。

雾气中传来一声低沉的"吱呀"声。接着是

一片寂静，随后又是"吱呀"一声。

丁丁大口大口地喘着气，僵在了那里。"声音越来越近了！"他小声地说。

"说……说不定是海……海盗呢！"乔希说。

"也许就是那个长着一双大脚的家伙！"露丝说，"说不定这就是他埋藏的宝藏！"

"咱们快离开这里吧！"丁丁说，"快帮我把这扇门关好！"

孩子们把水泥门关上了。乔希抓起铁锹，丁

丁和露丝把塑料毒葛放回原处。现在,这个水泥箱又隐藏起来了。

丁丁带领小伙伴快速穿过巨石堆,原路返回河边。

狭窄的沙滩上,孩子们站在雾中倾听着。

丁丁又一次听到"吱呀"的声音,然后是轻轻的"砰"的一声,紧接着就是一片寂静。

一条小船从雾中缓缓地漂了出来。一个魁梧的黑影弯腰坐在船尾。丁丁不敢动,也不敢出声。那个人好像正在盯着他们看呢!

时间过得很慢,好似过了一整年,那个人才划船离开。丁丁听到船桨划动时的"吱呀"声,小船又消失在了雾气中。

"那……那是谁啊?"乔希问道,声音低沉沙哑。

"我不知道。"丁丁回答道。

"管他是谁呢,咱们赶紧离开这座小岛吧!"露丝说。

于是孩子们静悄悄地踏入低浅的河水中。他们蹚水来到岸边,尽量不溅起水花。丁丁一直留

意着那条船,以及船上那个寂静无声的划船人。不过,在雾气中,他什么也没看见。

少女岛又一次消失在他们身后。

十分钟后,他们推开了法伦警官办公室的门。

法伦警官从电脑后面抬起头来。"怎么啦,孩子们?你们脸上的表情看着像是撞见了鬼!"

他盯着他们湿漉漉的运动鞋,说:"你们都湿透了!"

"我们刚才又发现了钱。"露丝说,"好几百万美元呢!"

法伦警官扬起了一侧的眉毛。

"是真的,我们真的发现了!"乔希说。

"好吧,坐下来跟我说说吧。"法伦警官一边说,一边关上了电脑。

孩子们挨着椅子边坐了下来。

"我们又去小岛了，"丁丁解释道，"并且发现了一个水泥做的保险箱。里面装着一摞又一摞的钱呢！"

他们把那条隐蔽的小路、塑料做的毒葛，还有被藏起来的那个水泥金库的事全都告诉了法伦警官。

"就在我们刚要离开小岛的时候，我们看见有人划着小船过去了。"乔希说，"我觉得他是要到小岛上去的，不过随后他又掉头离开了！"

法伦警官坐直了身子。"你们看清楚那个人了吗？"他问孩子们。

"雾太大了。"丁丁说。

法伦警官皱了皱眉头，接着又点了点头。

"为什么会有人在少女岛上藏钱呢？"露丝不解地问，"他们为什么不把钱存在普通的银行里呢？"

法伦警官看着露丝。"因为藏在那里的钱都不是真钱。"他说。

"不是真钱？"露丝问，"那是什么？"

"我觉得我没有理由不告诉你们了。"法伦警官说,"你们昨天离开以后,我想起了几周之前读到的关于制造假钞的报道。于是我仔细看了看你们捡到的那张钞票。"

他从抽屉里抽出那个信封,拿出那张百元大钞。"这是一张假钞,孩子们。我猜,你们这次在水泥保险箱里看到的钱也是假钞。"

"假钞?"乔希倒吸了一口气,"您的意思是,所有的钱都是假钞吗?"

法伦警官笑了。"很遗憾,是的,乔希。"

"可是,是谁把假钞藏在那里的呢?"丁丁不解地问道。

"这正是我们现在要查明的。"法伦警官说。

他站起身来送孩子们到门边。"基恩警官和我今天会去那里看一看。从现在开始,我们会一直派人监视那座小岛。"

法伦警官打开办公室的门。"现在你们可以走了。不过,你们要跟我保证,离那座小岛远远的。制造假钞的人很危险!"

孩子们谢过法伦警官后就离开了。他们走在

主街的时候，丁丁心里想着之前看到的船上的那个神秘身影。他就是制造假钞的那个人吗？他看见他们三个站在沙滩上了吗？

丁丁不禁咽了口唾沫。他、乔希和露丝会有危险吗？

第七章

乔希先是挠了挠他的膝盖,然后是他的脖子,接着是左边手肘。

"我想我最好还是去买点炉甘石药膏。"他说。

"咱们就快到超市了。"丁丁一边说,一边朝身后瞥了一眼。

"你在看什么?"露丝问他。

丁丁耸了耸肩。"没什么。我想,我只是心里一直想着船上那个令人毛骨悚然的家伙。"

"你觉得他认出咱们了吗?"乔希问道,"我的意思是,既然咱们看不清他的脸,说不定他也看不清咱们的脸。"

"希望你说得没错。"丁丁说,"如果船上那个家伙就是制造假钞的人,他可能是任何人,甚至是我们之前认识的人!"

"哎呀,你可真行,大坏蛋。"乔希说,"这下我可要做噩梦了!"

这时,孩子们走进超市,朝着药品柜台走去。埃尔南德斯太太抬起头,朝他们笑了笑。

"嘿,孩子们,想要点什么?"她问道。

乔希挠着膝盖。"您这里有炉甘石药膏吗?"他问道。

隐形岛

　　埃尔南德斯太太从柜台后面走了出来，匆匆地给乔希检查了一下。

　　"毫无疑问，这是毒葛划伤的。"她一边说，一边从架子上取下一个粉色瓶子递给乔希，"这可是我这里的最后一瓶了。罗恩·平科夫斯基昨天过来把另外三瓶都买走了。"

　　乔希付了钱，给埃尔南德斯太太道了谢。随后，孩子们离开了超市。他们在一条长凳上坐下来，乔希把炉甘石药膏涂抹在身上发痒的地方。

"我在想，平先生为什么需要这种东西。"露丝说，"之前他不是告诉我们，他对毒葛是避而远之的吗？"

"昨天我们看见他的时候没看到他在身上抓挠啊。"丁丁说。

突然，乔希跳起来。"我的天哪！是他！"

丁丁四下里看了看。"是谁？"

"平先生啊！"乔希说，"他被毒葛划伤了，所以去买了炉甘石药膏。因为他去少女岛藏假钞，所以他被毒葛划伤了。"

丁丁摇了摇头。"就算平先生的确被毒葛划伤了，也可能是在其他地方被毒葛划伤的。"

"说不定他在哪个空鱼缸里藏着一台印刷机呢！"乔希说。

"乔希，你在说什么呢！"露丝说。

"我的推理堪称完美！"乔希说，"他卖鱼饵是为了遮人耳目，他发财真正靠的是制造假钞！"

"你太不理智了。"丁丁说，"咱们不能仅仅因为平先生买了炉甘石药膏就断定他是制造假钞的人吧。"

乔希把药膏的盖子拧好,塞进口袋里。"我才没有不理智呢!"他说,"他个子高,所以很可能脚也大,对不对?"

露丝张开嘴巴,正要开口说话,乔希却打断了她。

"而且,他正好住在河边。"乔希接着说,"他自己正好有船!他知道少女岛是个藏钱的理想之地。肯定是他干的!"

丁丁看着露丝。"你是怎么想的?"他问。

"船上的那个人有可能是平先生。"露丝说,"可是,他是我们的朋友。我不相信他会是那个制造假钞的人。"

"我也不相信。"丁丁说。

"好吧,我相信!"乔希一边说,一边挠着自己的肚皮,"咱们再去趟鱼饵店,看看他身上是不是有毒葛划伤的痕迹吧。"

"可是,我们怎么才能知道他有没有被划伤呢?"露丝问道,既不解又好奇。

乔希咧着嘴笑了。"他买了三瓶炉甘石药膏哟。"他提醒露丝,"他身上肯定有粉色的痕迹!"

丁丁哈哈大笑起来。"好吧，咱们去鱼饵店吧。"他说，"你负责寻找他身上被毒葛划伤的痕迹。我倒是想看看平先生的两只脚是不是和那些脚印一样大！"

第八章

"嗯,有一件事你猜得没错。"露丝小声地对乔希说,"平先生确实长着一双大脚!"

"没错,不过,他的脚看起来还是没有我们之前看到的那些脚印大。"丁丁小声地回应。

孩子们躲在罗恩鱼饵店附近的灌木丛后面。此时罗恩站在院子里,正在用一块布擦着一条绿色的小船。

"快看那条船!"乔希说,"它很可能就是之前我们在小岛上看到的那条呢!"

"不过我没看见他身上有任何炉甘石药膏的痕迹。"丁丁说,"而且,他也没有挠身上的任何地方啊！"

这时，一辆黑色汽车开进了他家的车道。一个身穿深色套装的人从车里走下来，罗恩朝他挥了挥手。

那个人也朝罗恩挥了挥手，随即把身子探进车里，取出来一个箱子。箱子的一侧写着四个大字：开心狗粮！

乔希倒吸了一口气，说："你们看见——"

"嘘！"露丝小声地提醒着。

随后，孩子们看见那个人把箱子递给了罗恩。罗恩转身把箱子搬进了他的小屋。

隐形岛

不一会儿，罗恩从屋子里出来了。他把箱子还给了那个陌生人，陌生人把箱子放在他的汽车座椅上，拿出一本支票簿，匆匆开具了一张支票递给罗恩。

最后，他钻进自己的汽车，开车离开了。

"赶快把车牌号记下来！"露丝说。

丁丁开口念出了车牌号。"B-E-N-T，BENT？是什么意思？"他问道。

"管它什么意思呢。"乔希说，"我们只知道平先生把满满一箱子假钞卖给了那个家伙！咱们去告诉法伦警官吧！"

"乔希，那个箱子里面很可能装满了狗粮。"丁丁说。

"大笨蛋，你好好想想吧！"乔希说，"有人把假钞藏在少女岛的那些装狗粮的箱子里。我敢打赌，这两个家伙中肯定有一个是制造假钞的！"

A to Z 神秘案件

"可能乔希说得没错。"露丝说,"不过,告诉法伦警官之前,说不定咱们可以查出来那个人是谁。"

"怎么查?"丁丁问。

"咱们去加油站问问吧。"露丝说,"霍利先生可能知道谁开着车牌号为 BENT 的黑色汽车。"

当孩子们到达加油站时,却没见着霍利先生的人影。

随后,丁丁听见有人吹口哨的声音。口哨声是从一辆被撞毁的红色皮卡车下面传出来的。

"霍利先生?"丁丁问道,"是您吗?"

这时一张沾满油污的圆圆的脸从皮卡车下面探出来。

"你们好,"霍利先生一边跟孩子们打招呼,一边朝孩子们咧着嘴笑,"你们有关于车子的问题吗?"

"算是吧。"露丝说,"您知道车牌号为 BENT 的汽车是谁的吗?"

霍利先生站起来,在一块抹布上擦了擦手。

"哎呀,车子变形了[1]?"他一边问,一边朝丁丁眨巴着眼睛。

丁丁哈哈大笑起来。"不是的,不过我们需要找到开那辆车的人。"他说。

"我捡到了一些钱。"露丝说,"我们觉得可能是他的。"

"听上去好像是那两个刚搬来的人,"霍利先生说,"沃登·本特先生和他的太太。几周前,他们在狐狸小道租了一栋小房子。我给他们那辆时髦的林肯汽车更换过火花塞。"

"狐狸小道!"丁丁一边说,一边看了乔希一眼,"就在靠近河边的地方啊!"

"没错。"霍利先生说,"河边景色很美。不

---

1. 英文单词 BENT 的含义之一为"变形的"。——译者

好意思，我现在要去修这辆旧卡车了！"

孩子们谢过霍利先生，离开了加油站。

"现在，咱们知道那个家伙是谁了。"丁丁说，"可是，我们还是无法证明他或者平先生就是制造假钞的人啊。"

"但是那个箱子——"乔希开口说。

"咱们不知道里面装的是什么。"丁丁提醒他。

"没错。"露丝说，"咱们为什么不去一趟本特先生家呢？等他进屋时，说不定咱们能偷看一眼那个箱子里面装的是什么东西呢。"

"好吧，不过咱们得小心谨慎。"丁丁说，"我可不想被锁进少女岛的那个金库里！"

第九章

孩子们穿过蓟花街朝狐狸小道走去。

狭窄的巷子里只有三栋小房子。最后一栋是一个小屋,几乎隐藏在树木和茂密的灌木丛中。不知哪个地方还会时而传来"啾啾"的鸟叫声。

乔希轻轻推了推丁丁。"看,那辆汽车!"他小声地说着,用手指着一个方向。

树底下停放着的正是孩子们先前看到的那辆黑色汽车,车牌号是BENT。

孩子们偷偷地溜到汽车旁边。三个人透过车子的后窗玻璃往里面瞧。

汽车座位上和地板上都没有写着"开心狗粮"的箱子。

"肯定是被他搬进家里了。"丁丁一边说,一边在乔希和露丝旁边蹲了下来。

"现在咱们该怎么办啊?"乔希问道。

"咱们得想办法进到他家里。"露丝说。

乔希看着她。"怎么进去?"

"按响门铃,说咱们是卖女童子军饼干的,怎么样?"

乔希翻了个白眼,不以为然。"想什么呢,两个男孩在卖女童子军饼干!"

"好吧,那我一个人去吧。"露丝说。

"不行。"丁丁说,"谁也不能进那栋房子。如果本特夫妇是制造假钞的人,那他们就是危险分子!"

"那咱们怎么办啊?"乔希问道,"咱们假装卖三明治吧,我觉得这一招肯定行得通!"

突然,房子的前门打开了。一只短腿猎犬耷拉着耳朵,摇摇摆摆地走到门廊上。这只猎犬长着棕白相间的毛,一双大大的眼睛里流露出忧伤的神情。

"待在家附近别走远,矮冬瓜!"有人说道。

"哎呀。"乔希小声说。

"趁它还没觉察到我们来了,赶紧离开这里吧!"露丝说。

孩子们消失在小屋两旁疯长的浓密灌木丛中。他们蹑手蹑脚地朝后院走去,尽量不弄出任何声响。

"快看!"丁丁指着小屋后面的一个小车库说。除了门,小车库周围都是灌木丛。"我们可以躲到那里去!"

这时,猎犬大叫了一声。

露丝扭过头,往后面看去。"哎呀,不好了!它在追我们!"

孩子们飞快地冲到车库后面。丁丁在那里发现了一扇低矮的窗户。

"快进去!"他一边说,一边把窗扇推了上去。

猎犬绕过墙角,大步跑过来,同时用鼻子嗅着地面。

"狗狗真乖。"乔希小声地说。

猎犬看了一眼乔希,又叫了一声。

"快,到里面来!"丁丁一边说,一边纵身跳进被打开的窗户。

乔希和露丝也一拥而上跳进车库,压在了丁丁身上。外面的猎犬开始"汪汪汪"地叫起来。丁丁看到了猎犬黑色的口鼻,还看到它两只眼睛从窗台上往里面张望。于是他把乔希从身上推开,随即关上了窗户。

隐形岛

猎犬还在"汪汪汪"地叫着,用它的两只大爪子挠着窗户。

"我们必须藏起来!"丁丁说,"这么大的声音。本特夫妇肯定能听见!"

孩子们迅速往四周看了看。墙脚放着一个工作台,上面堆满了杂物。丁丁注意到工作台的对面有一堆盖着一层防水布的杂物。

乔希和露丝钻到工作台下面。丁丁径直朝

防水布走去。他掀开防水布的一个角，爬到下面；接着放下防水布，让它垂落下来，盖在自己背上。

防水布下面黑乎乎的，丁丁什么也看不见。他感觉自己趴在几个硬箱子上面，箱子的边缘棱角分明，很硌人。

突然，猎犬不叫了。丁丁听到有人说话的声音。

他掀起防水布的一角朝窗户看去。透过脏兮兮的窗玻璃，丁丁看见一位女士的两条腿。她弯下腰，抱着猎犬走了。

丁丁连大气都不敢出，一直等到心里确定那位女士不会回来了，才从防水布下面爬了出来。乔希和露丝也从车库另一边的工作台下爬了出来。

"好险啊！"露丝说。

丁丁往四周看了看，发现他们几个正站在水泥地板上。空气凉爽干燥。车库的一个角落里放着一些园艺工具和几根鱼竿。

随后丁丁发现了一件东西。"快看！"他说。

工作台上放着一个"开心狗粮"的箱子。

"说不定这就是之前放在本特先生汽车里的那个箱子呢!"丁丁说。他猛地打开箱子的盖子,发现里面只有一个油漆罐,油漆罐边缘有绿色的污渍。

丁丁思忖了片刻,说:"两位,还记得平先生正在修理的那条船吗?船是绿色的,对吧?"

他拿起油漆罐。"说不定那条船是本特先生的呢,而罗恩帮他把船刷上了一层油漆。这可能就是用剩的油漆。"

"这么说,本特先生给他开具的支票就是给他的刷漆费啦!"露丝说。

她把手伸进箱子,掏出一个纸团,接着在工作台上把纸团展开压平。

"这是药店开具的一张收据,"露丝说,"买的是三瓶炉甘石药膏!"

丁丁盯着收据看了看。收据显示付款方式是信用卡支付。收据的底部清楚地印着一个名字:罗纳德·W.平科夫斯基。[1]

---

1. 罗恩·平科夫斯基的全名。——编者

"嘿，两位，咱们把这里好好地查一查！"

乔希已经在车库的另一边翻找起来了。墙上的挂钩上挂着两双绿色的长筒胶皮雨靴。

乔希解开其中一双雨靴的搭扣，把雨靴取下来。"快来看看这双雨靴的尺码！"他说。

丁丁走过去仔细看了看。

"少女岛上的那些大脚印，肯定是这双雨靴留下来的！"他说。

露丝仔细检查了其中一只雨靴的底部。鞋底的凹纹里塞满了小石子和沙子。

孩子们你看着我，我看着你。

"现在咱们该怎么办啊？"乔希问道。

"去把我们发现的情况报告给法伦警官。"丁丁说。

他踮起脚尖走到车库门边，透过门缝往外看。

"哎呀，"丁丁说，"咱们遇到麻烦了，两位。本特太太刚刚拿出来一些吃的。她正在烤架上点火呢！"

"很好。"乔希咕哝着，"我被困在这里，都快饿死了！"

他和露丝也凑到丁丁跟前，透过门缝往外看。

"快看！"露丝说。

这时，一个高个子男人来到烤架边。此人正是他们先前在罗恩鱼饵店见到的那个人。不过，他现在穿的是短裤和T恤衫。

他长长的胳膊和腿上涂满了炉甘石药膏。

第十章

露丝惊讶得低声倒抽了一口气。"原来他就是在少女岛被毒葛划伤的那个人!炉甘石药膏原来是买给他用的!"

"不过药可是平先生买的。"乔希说,"我还是觉得他们两个是一伙的!"

丁丁再次透过车库的门缝往外面看了看。"本特先生在看报纸,"他小声地说,"本特太太在烤汉堡包。"

"那条猎犬在吗?"乔希问道。

"在呢。"

"如果我们想要离开,那条猎犬很可能还会叫。"露丝说。

"汉堡包闻起来真是太香了!"乔希一边说,一边发出低低的哼哼声。

"别总是惦记吃的了,"丁丁说,"还是想想如何从这里逃出去吧!"

"好吧,我来想办法!"乔希一边说,一边把丁丁推到一边,自己朝门缝外面看。

"我想到了一个办法。"过了一会儿,他说。

"快告诉我们!"露丝说。

乔希咧着嘴笑了。"咱们邀请本特夫妇进车库里吧!"

露丝摇了摇头。"毒葛终于把他的脑子给毒傻了。"她对丁丁说。

"不,听我说。"乔希开口道,"咱们弄出些大的动静,本特夫妇和猎犬准能听到。他们一定会飞快地跑过来,看看究竟发生了什么事情,然后——"

"然后就在车库里把咱们抓住!"丁丁打断了他的话。

A to Z 神秘案件

乔希神秘地笑了。"不会的,因为我们可以从窗户跳出去。他们看不见我们的!"

丁丁点了点头,一副若有所思的表情。"这个办法可能管用。"他说,"不过,我觉得咱们应该想个办法,让他们待在里面的时间长一些,这样咱们就有足够的时间离开了。"

"我有个主意!"露丝走到工作台边。"这里面肯定有写字用的东西。"她喃喃道。

"你想要写什么啊?"乔希问道。

"啊哈!"露丝从工具箱里拿出一根木匠用的粉笔。

她跪在地板上,用大大的字写了下面的内容:

> 我知道了你们制造假钞的事情。咱们好好聊聊吧,不然我就去警察局报警了。一个小时后少女岛见。

"啊,我的天哪!"乔希尖叫起来。

"可是,如果他们去小岛拿走了钱,离开了镇子,怎么办呢?"丁丁问道。

"这样正好！他们做这些事情的时候，法伦警官正等着他们呢！"露丝说。

乔希在工具箱里发现了一把锤子。"给我找点东西来砸吧！"他对丁丁说，"然后随时准备逃跑啦！"

"我来负责盯着外面！"露丝一边说，一边朝车库门走去。

丁丁把车库扫视了一遍，然后走到自己之前藏身的防水布旁边。他猛地把防水布揭开，然后轻声地吹了一声口哨。"两位，快看！"

乔希和露丝匆忙跑过来。丁丁发现了四个"开心狗粮"的箱子。

丁丁揭开一个箱子的盖子，朝里面看。

"只是一罐一罐的狗粮。"他说。

"他肯定是用空箱子来装假钞。"露丝说。

这时，乔希发现了一个空桶。"我敢打赌，我可以用这个桶吸引他们的注意力！"他说。

丁丁打开了窗户。露丝走过去，站在他身边。"好了，乔希，"丁丁说，"开始吧！"

于是，乔希深深地吸了一口气，然后开始用

锤子重重地敲打空桶底部。

声音像雷声一样,从车库里传了出去。

"好了!"乔希说着,扔下锤子和空桶,快速朝窗户跑去。

孩子们从车库里跳出来,蹲伏在杂草丛中。几秒钟后,他们听到车库门打开时发出的"嘎吱"声,本特先生说:"待着别动,矮冬瓜!"

接着,丁丁听到本特太太说:"沃登,这里面有人来过。地板上写着字呢!"

这正是孩子们想听到的对话。他们朝房子另一边的树林跑去。两分钟过后,他们穿过了高中的运动场,径直朝主街跑去。

"多么希望法伦警官在办公室啊。"丁丁上气不接下气地说。

他真的在办公室呢。孩子们破门而入,满脸通红。

法伦警官抬起头。"你们这是——"

"我们发现了制造假钞的人!"三个孩子喊道。

第十一章

孩子们你不让我，我不让你，抢着把在本特夫妇家发现的情况告诉了法伦警官。

还没等孩子们说到"开心狗粮"的箱子，法伦警官就已经对着电话大声下达指示了。

"不要再去狐狸小道了！"说完这句话，他就奔向门口，消失不见了。

"现在怎么办？"丁丁问。

"咱们为什么要被落下？"露丝问道，"一起去看看吧。"

"去哪里啊？"乔希问道，"他说了不让去——"

"不是去狐狸小道。"丁丁打断了乔希的话,"这次的行动在少女岛展开哟!"

几分钟后,孩子们在沿河路上法伦警官的巡逻警车旁喘着气休息。这时,雾气已经消散,他们可以更清楚地看见少女岛了。

丁丁朝河的对岸望去,但是只望到了沙子和岩石。

乔希累得上气不接下气,瘫倒在地上。"我想我累得心脏病都要发作了!"他呻吟着。

"你们觉得法伦警官在那里吗?"露丝一边问,一边眯着眼睛看向河对面,"一个人我都没看见呢。"

孩子们坐在巡逻警车的阴影里,盯着小岛。

突然,乔希跳了起来。"他们在那儿!"他大喊了一声。

三个身影从小岛的另一边走了过来。距离太远了,孩子们看不清他们都是谁,不过丁丁认为自己看清了法伦警官的深色警服。

接着,第四个人出现了,他身后拖着一条小小的平底船。

"那是法伦警官和基恩警官!"丁丁说,"他们把本特夫妇抓住了!"

孩子们看着这群人越来越近。河里的水快到法伦警官的膝盖处了,他走在最前头,后面跟着戴着手铐的本特夫妇。基恩警官拖着船走在后面。那是一条绿色的小船!

"看看船里都有什么吧!"乔希说,"里面堆满了钱和狗粮箱子呢!"

法伦警官领着两个制造假钞的人走向河岸边,一路上谁也没有开口说话。本特夫妇穿着长筒胶皮雨靴,跌跌撞撞地上了河岸,脸上露出愤怒的表情。

基恩警官将小船拉上岸,把假钞放进巡逻警车的后备厢。法伦警官替本特夫妇打开警车后门。等到本特夫妇进入车内,法伦警官把车门锁上了。

"干得漂亮!"他一边赞扬孩子们,一边看着乔希:"你爸爸妈妈在家吗?"

"我不知道。"乔希回答道。

"一个小时之后在你家等着我。"法伦警官

说。随后他和基恩警官挽起他们湿漉漉的长裤裤腿,钻进了巡逻警车。

警车疾驰而去,空气中扬起一片灰尘和松针。

"法伦警官为什么要找你爸爸妈妈啊?"丁丁一边问,一边咧着嘴笑,"你惹麻烦了吧?"

"哇,我在想监狱里的食物是什么样子的!"露丝说。

丁丁拍了拍乔希的肚皮。"我听说他们给囚犯吃的早餐是蠕虫做的华夫饼呢!"

"嘻嘻,"乔希说,"你们太搞笑了!因为我逮着了本特夫妇,他很可能想要给我一笔奖励。"

"不是你一个人逮着的,"露丝提醒他,"是咱们三个一起逮着的!"

"可是大家都知道,我在咱们团队中是最聪明的一个。"乔希笑着说。

他们穿过一片田野来到了乔希家。乔希猛地把后门拉开,大声喊道:"有人在家吗?"

没有人回答他。"咱们吃点东西吧。"乔希

说,"我来做一些三明治。"

他们坐在乔希家的后院里,手里拿着果冻三明治、纸杯和一罐牛奶。

"我很好奇,本特夫妇制造假钞的地方在哪里。"丁丁问道,"你们觉得那栋房子里是不是藏着一台印刷机?"

乔希放下手里的三明治。"需要钱用,随时可以制造出来,这是一种什么样的感觉啊?"

这时,丁丁听到汽车驶入乔希家车道的声音。随后车门"砰"的一声关上了,是法伦警官来了。

"你的牛奶能给我喝点吗?"他问乔希。

"当然可以啦!"乔希倒了一杯牛奶递给法伦警官。

他喝了一大口牛奶,然后看着孩子们。"本特夫妇被关起来了,但他们什么都不肯交代。不过就算他们开口说话,我想我们也只能查出来他们不过是中间人而已。印刷这些百元大钞的人还在某个地方逍遥法外呢。"

"可是,本特夫妇为什么要把假钞藏在少女

岛呢?"乔希不解地问。

"去那儿很方便啊。"法伦警官解释道,"由于他们的船就寄放在鱼饵店,他们划船过去,几分钟的时间就能到小岛上。"

"一开始,我们以为平先生可能跟他们是一伙的。"丁丁说。

法伦警官点了点头。"我明白你们为什么会这样想。我找罗恩了解过了,他们确实把船放在了他的院子里。后来,本特在少女岛看见你们几个之后,又请罗恩给船刷了一层漆。我猜他是担心你们再看到那条船会认出来。"

"平先生为什么要买炉甘石药膏?"乔希问。

"罗恩人很好。"法伦警官说,"我猜是他注意到本特痒得难受,所以就给他买了药膏。"

这时,法伦警官瞥了一眼乔希家的牲口棚。"那里面养着什么动物吗?"他问乔希。

"没有。"乔希说,"我和我那对双胞胎弟弟本来想养一匹小马,可是我爸爸说养马太麻烦了。"

"养条宠物狗怎么样?"法伦警官说,"我碰巧有一条很温顺的短腿猎犬,它正需要一个友好的家。"

听到这话,乔希的眼睛一下子亮了起来。"是真的吗?"

法伦警官笑了笑。"或许你们两个应该相互认识认识。"

于是他吹了声口哨。基恩警官牵着一条耷拉着耳朵的短腿猎犬,从拐角处小跑过来。

"原来是矮冬瓜啊!"露丝惊讶地说。

"你们已经认识这条狗了?"法伦警官问道。

"它当时在本特家,"丁丁解释道,"它差点就把我们的藏身之地给暴露了!"

法伦警官抚摸着猎犬天鹅绒般丝滑的耳朵。"它的主人要坐很长时间的牢。它需要一个新家。"

乔希跪下来,拍了拍猎犬丝滑柔软的皮毛。

"嘿,狗狗。"他跟猎犬打着招呼,"你想住在这儿吗?"

猎犬伸出长长的粉色舌头舔了舔乔希,然后"扑通"一声重重地卧倒在地,打了个滚。

"它喜欢我!"乔希说。

"我正指望着这个呢,那就拜托你啦。"法伦警官一边说,一边把拴狗绳交到乔希手里,随即往他的警车走去。"回头叫你爸爸妈妈给我打个电话哟!"说完,他便离开了。

"谢谢您,法伦警官!"乔希大声地说。

"咱们该给它取个什么名字呢?"过了一会儿,乔希问道。

"它已经有名字了,"露丝提醒乔希,"叫矮冬瓜。"

乔希摇了摇头。"这个名字太难听了。如果你长得矮,你会喜欢大家叫你矮冬瓜吗?"

"乔希说得没错,"丁丁说,"咱们可以想一个比这个更好听的名字。"

可是,一个小时过去了,乔希的爸爸妈妈回家了,孩子们还没有给猎犬选出一个好名字来。

当乔希终于得到爸爸妈妈的允许,可以养这条猎犬时,狗狗仍然没有名字。

那天晚上的晚些时间,丁丁、乔希和露丝各自回到自己的卧室睡觉去了。

A to Z 神秘案件

那只耷拉着耳朵的短腿猎犬在乔希的床尾打起了呼噜。

不过,它还是没有名字。

A to Z Mysteries®

The Invisible Island

by Ron Roy

illustrated by
John Steven Gurney

INDIAN RIVER
LAWRENCE TAXI
RIVER ROAD
HORSE TRAILS
HORSES FOR RENT
BIKE PATH
WOODS
WOODVIEW ROAD
INDIAN WAY ROAD
FIRE STATION
BILL'S BIKES
SUPER MARKET
BRIDGE LANE
ROBIN ROAD
CROW ST
FINCH LA
THRUSH CT
OWL RD
PHEASANT LA
BLUE JAY WAY
WREN DR
FITNESS CENTER
WOODS
BIKE PATH
BLUE BIRD WAY
HUMMINGBIRD LA
WOODCOCK CROSS
ELLIE'S DINER
ACORN APTS
FURRY FEET PET SHOP
OAK STREET
CENTER CHURCH
BIKE PATH
PEOPLE'S POND
POST OFFICE
COMMUNITY GARDEN AND FISH POND
GREEN LAWN $ SAVINGS BANK $
POLICE STATION
ELDERLY HOUSING
GOOSE ISLAND
RIVER ROAD
WEST GREEN ST
SENIOR COMMUNITY CENTER
GREEN LAWN LIBRARY
TOWN HALL
MAIN STREET
BIKE PATH
CHILDREN'S PETTING ZOO AND AQUARIUM
SHANGRI-LA HOTEL

WELCOME TO
GREEN LAWN
HOME OF THE
A to Z Mysteries
N
W
E
S
RIVER ROAD
BOAT LAUNCH
SQUAW ISLAND
BOAT RENTAL
RON'S BAIT
GREEN LAWN MIDDLE SCHOOL
DUCK WALK WAY
EAGLE LANE
FARM LANE
JOSH
GREEN LAWN ELEMENTARY SCHOOL
DINK
RUTH ROSE
TREE TOP CIRCLE
MEADOW ROAD
FOX LANE
QUAIL RUN ROAD
SILVER CIRCLE
WOODY STREET
PLEASANT STREET
BAND SHELL
ROSE GARDEN
THISTLE COURT
WILDFLOWER WAY
CENTER PARK
ROSE STREET
GREEN LAWN HIGH SCHOOL
SWAN POND
PLAYING FIELDS
GYM + POOL
BOXWOOD LANE
HOWARD'S BARBER-SHOP
BOOK NOOK
GAS STATION
CRYSTAL POND
MYSTIC GREENHOUSE
DOG KENNEL + VETERINARIAN
RIVER ROAD
EAST GREEN STREET
TOWN TENNIS COURTS
TOWN SWIMMING POOL
KIDDIE POOL
TOWN BASEBALL FIELD
TO THE BLUE HILLS

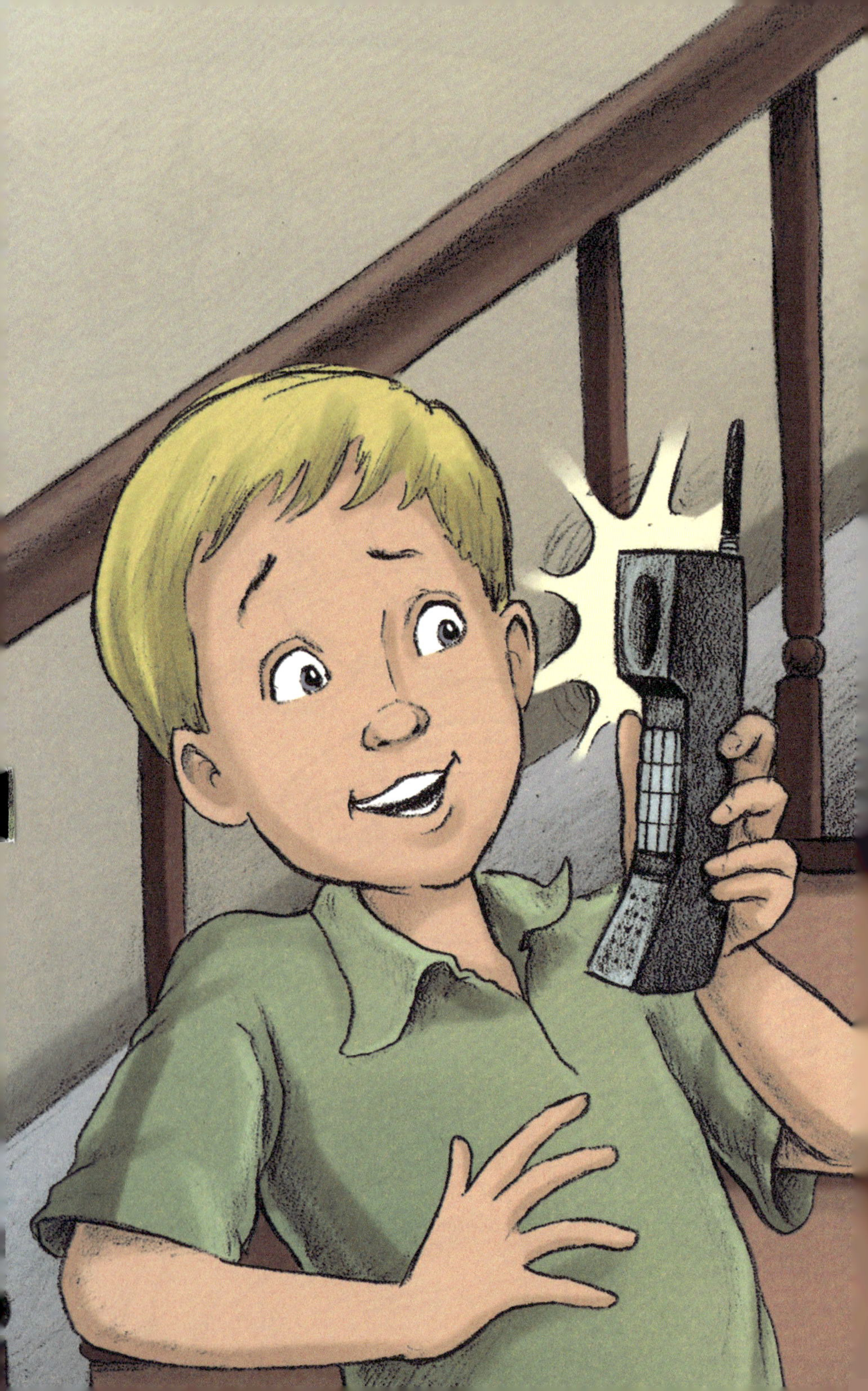

Chapter 1

Donald David Duncan, known as Dink to his friends, answered the telephone.

"Duncan residence, Dink speaking."

"Get over here!" Josh Pinto yelled.

Dink jerked the phone away from his ear. "Why?" he asked.

"My mom says we can have a picnic on Squaw Island," Josh said. "She made us lunch!"

It was a steaming hot July day.

Splashing around in the Indian River would feel great, thought Dink.

"Okay, let me tell my mom and pick up Ruth Rose. We'll be right over."

Dink ran up the stairs to his parents' room. His mother was sitting at her sewing machine, mending a pair of Dink's jeans.

"Hey, Mom? Me and Josh and Ruth Rose are going to the river for a picnic, okay?" Dink asked.

"Okay, but you kids stay together," she said.

"Thanks, Mom!" Dink pulled on old shorts and his grubbiest sneakers. Before he left, he fed Loretta, his guinea pig. Dink heard her squeak happily as he ran back down the stairs.

Dink hurried over to Ruth Rose's house. Ruth Rose's cat, Tiger, was nursing her kittens on the front step. Dink carefully stepped around them, then rang the bell.

The door opened. Ruth Rose's little brother, Nate, stood in the doorway. He had a cookie in each hand and another in his mouth.

"Hi, Natie," Dink said. "Is your sister here?"

"Shu goofen muppy," Nate said through his cookie.

Dink blinked at Nate. "Huh?"

Ruth Rose appeared next to Nate. "Hi, Dink, what's going on?" she said.

Ruth Rose Hathaway liked to dress all in one color. Today she wore blue shorts, a blue T-shirt, and blue sneakers. Her springy black curls were held in place by a blue headband.

"Josh wants to go to Squaw Island for a picnic," Dink said.

Ruth Rose grinned. "Great!" She leaned back into the house. "SEE YOU LATER, MOM! I'M GOING ON A PICNIC WITH THE GUYS!"

Then she bent down and wiped cookie crumbs from her brother's lips. "Natie, go stay with Mommy, okay? I'll bring you back a magic stone!"

Nate grinned and ran back into the house.

Ruth Rose pulled the door shut. Then she and Dink cut through her backyard and crossed Eagle Lane. A few minutes later, they were at Josh's house.

Josh was in his front yard, holding a garden hose. His little twin brothers, Brian and Bradley, were screaming and racing through the water.

"Hi," Josh said when he saw Dink and Ruth Rose. He shut off the water.

"Gotta go," he told Brian and Bradley. "Be good boys and don't leave the yard!"

Josh grabbed his backpack off the porch. "Hope you guys're hungry," he said. "Mom packed a lot of food."

"That should last you about three minutes!" Dink said, grinning.

The kids hiked through the field behind Josh's house. Then they crossed River Road and walked to the bank of the Indian River.

The river flowed slowly, rippling over a few large rocks. In most places, the water was shallow enough to wade across. Trees and shrubbery grew along the banks. Birds and squirrels chattered in the greenery.

The kids walked along the river, slapping at mosquitoes. They stopped when they saw Squaw Island.

The small island sat in the middle of the river. It was mostly sand, shrubs, and rocks. No trees grew there, and no animals made the island their home. But the kids loved the sandy beach and clean, shallow water.

They waded in, wearing their sneakers. Soon they were up to their knees.

"Boy, this feels good!" Dink said as the cool water climbed his sweaty legs. He kicked water at Josh and Ruth Rose. They splashed him back, and pretty soon all three were soaked.

A few minutes later, they flopped down on the island's small beach. Dink took off his sneakers and wiggled his toes in the warm sand.

"Let's eat!" Josh said. He opened his backpack and brought out plastic bags holding sandwiches, slices of watermelon, and cookies.

"I wonder what it would be like to be stranded on an island," he said.

Dink chewed his sandwich. "Josh, we couldn't get stranded out here. All we'd have to do is wade back to shore."

Josh had a faraway look in his eyes. "Yeah, but what if pirates buried treasure here?" he said. He dug a hole in the sand with his heel. "We could be sitting over a chest filled with gold!"

"I don't think there were any pirates in Connecticut," Ruth Rose pointed out.

"Why not?" Josh asked. He gestured toward the vine-covered boulders in the center of the island. "This would be a perfect place for a pirate hideout!"

"Ahoy, mate!" Dink said.

Ruth Rose stood up. "I want to explore," she said. She walked toward the water. "I promised Nate I'd bring him a magic stone."

"What's a magic stone?" Dink asked. He followed her to the water's edge.

"This is!" Ruth Rose held up a smooth, pure white pebble.

"What makes it magic?"

"Nate has a bunch of these in his room," Ruth Rose said. "My parents told him if he kept his room neat, the stones would turn into nickels."

Josh joined Dink and Ruth Rose. He handed each

of them a cookie. "And Nate believed them?"

Ruth Rose grinned. "When Nate cleans his room, Mom sneaks in and takes one of the stones! She leaves a nickel in its place."

The kids started walking along the shore. The sun felt hot on Dink's back, so he took off his shirt.

"Hey, guys, look!" Josh yelled. He was standing over a footprint. "Somebody else has been here!"

He grinned at Dink and Ruth Rose. "Maybe it was Blackbeard!"

Dink stepped into the footprint. It was twice as big as his foot!

"I don't know about Blackbeard," he said, "but whoever this was has really big feet!"

"Look, here's another one!" Ruth Rose said. "And another!"

The kids followed the footprints away from the water. They led toward the boulders at the center of the island.

The footprints stopped suddenly in front of a squat, vine-covered boulder.

"That's funny," Dink said. "What'd the guy do,

jump over these rocks?"

"Maybe he walked around them," Josh said.

Dink and Josh began to circle the boulders slowly, looking for more footprints.

Ruth Rose started walking in the other direction. Suddenly, Dink heard her yell, "HEY, GUYS! COME OVER HERE QUICK!"

Dink and Josh ran back the way they'd come.

"Look!" Ruth Rose said, pointing down between her feet. Something green was poking out of the sand.

"What is it?" Josh asked.

"MONEY!" Ruth Rose yelled.

Chapter 2

"A ten-dollar bill!" Josh said, grabbing the bill and holding it up.

"Wrong," Dink said, plucking it out of Josh's fingers. "Count the zeroes!"

Josh's mouth fell open.

Ruth Rose's blue eyes got huge.

Dink was holding a hundred-dollar bill!

"A hundred bucks!" Josh squeaked.

He reached for the bill, but Dink quickly handed the money to Ruth Rose.

"She found it," he said.

"But who lost it?" Ruth Rose asked, shoving the

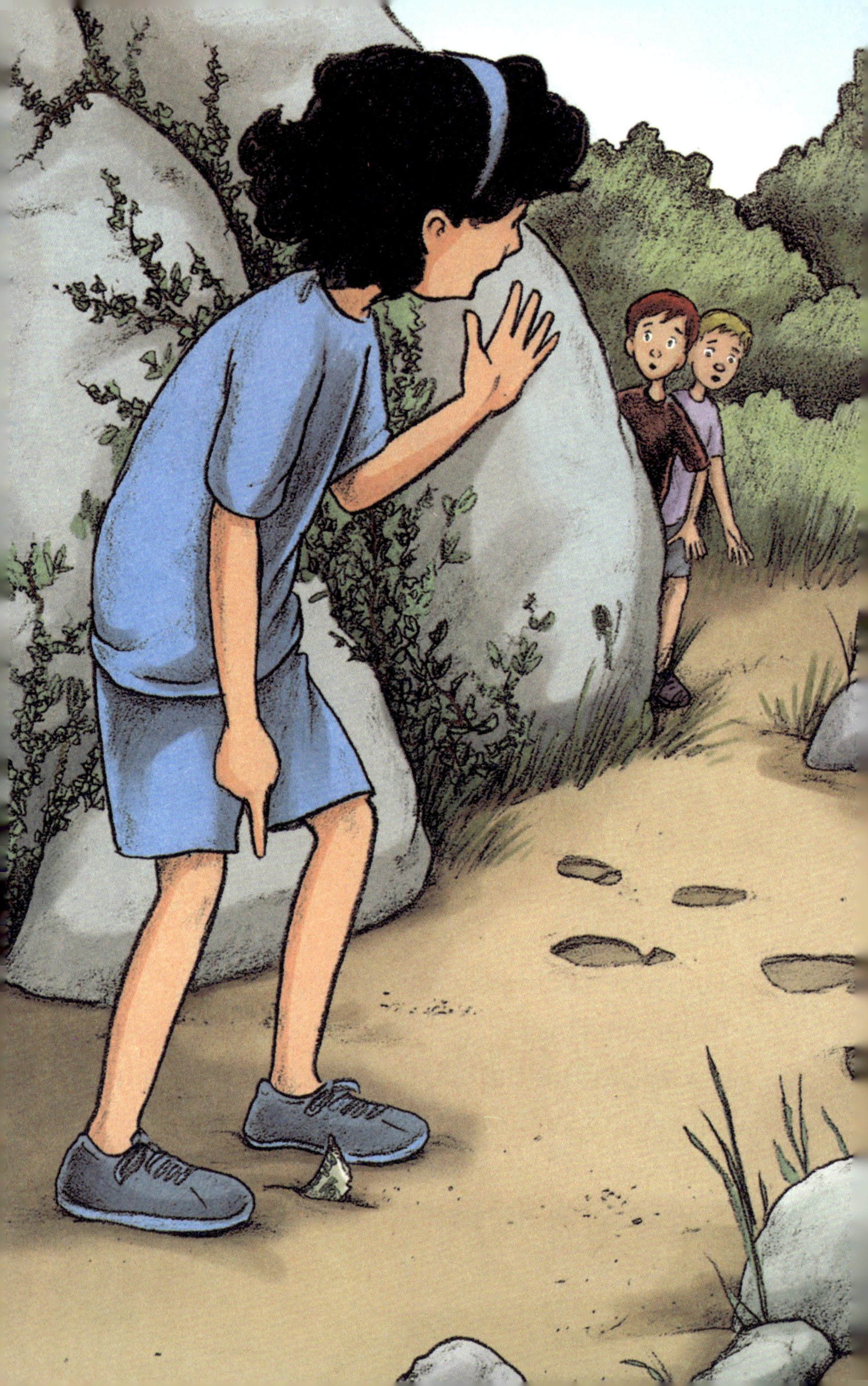

bill into a pocket.

Dink pointed to the footprints in the sand. "Maybe he did."

The kids stared at the footprints.

"Maybe he lost more," Josh said. "Let's search!"

The kids separated. With their eyes on the ground, they climbed over boulders and peeked under bushes. They found plenty of poison ivy, but no more hundred-dollar bills.

"Hey, guys, look at this," Dink called from near the water's edge.

Josh and Ruth Rose ran to where he was standing.

Dink pointed to a long patch of sand that was perfectly smooth. It looked as if someone had scraped a board over the sand, flattening all the little bumps.

"I'll bet somebody came out here with a rowboat," Ruth Rose said. "This must be where they dragged it up on the beach."

"I wonder if the same person who brought the boat made those footprints," Dink said, pulling his T-shirt back on.

"And dropped that hundred-dollar bill," said Josh.

Ruth Rose patted her pocket. "I don't know, but we have to try to find him."

"Why?" Josh said, grinning. "Think of what we could buy with that money. Split three ways, of course!"

"Forget it, Josh," Ruth Rose said. "The money isn't ours. We have to return it."

"To who?"

"To whoever lost it," Dink said.

"And how are we supposed to find the guy?" Josh asked.

The kids sat in the sand and thought.

"I know," Ruth Rose said. "We can go to Ron's Bait Shop. Maybe Mr. P knows who was out here."

"Good idea," Dink said.

"Boy," said Josh, getting to his feet. "You guys sure wanna get rid of that money fast."

"How would you feel if you lost a hundred-dollar bill?" Ruth Rose asked Josh.

He grinned. "Trust me, if I ever got one, I'd never lose it! Anyway, let's eat the watermelon my mom packed. Those cookies made my mouth dry."

They walked back to Josh's pack and slurped on sweet, juicy chunks of watermelon. They spit the seeds at each other as they packed up.

Josh shrugged into his backpack. "Well, if we have to return the money, maybe we'll get our names in the paper," he said. He scratched his ankles. "Maybe we'll get a reward!"

Ruth Rose giggled. "Josh, the only thing you're going to get is poison ivy!"

Chapter 3

  The kids waded back into the river. A few minutes later, they were squishing their way up River Road to Ron's Bait Shop.

  Ron Pinkowski lived in an old house next to the river. On the ground floor, he sold bait, boating supplies, and groceries. He also repaired and painted boats and fixed boat motors.

  The kids trudged down a dusty driveway to the house. Several small boats were lined up in Mr.

Pinkowski's big yard along the riverbank. A striped cat slept on the back step. Out the back door trailed a long orange extension cord. The kids followed the cord around the side of the house.

They spotted Mr. Pinkowski under a shady tree, sanding a boat bottom.

"Hi, Mr. P," Dink said.

Ron Pinkowski switched off the electric sander.

He was tall and sandyhaired, and sported a curly beard and droopy mustache.

"Well, hi, kids. What're you up to today?" he asked, smiling.

Ruth Rose pulled the hundred-dollar bill out of her pocket. "I just found this on Squaw Island," she said.

"Goodness," Ron said. "Aren't you a lucky gal!"

"We saw some marks in the sand from a boat," Dink said.

"And some footprints, too," Josh added. "Really big ones!"

"We think whoever was out there might have lost the money," Ruth Rose said.

"Hmm, wonder who it coulda been." Ron leaned against the boat and tugged on his beard. "Not many folks go out there. The poison ivy grows somethin' fierce in all that sand."

"Yeah, and I think I walked right through some!" Josh said, scratching his leg.

Ron smiled. "All I have to do is look at the stuff and I swell up like a balloon," he said.

"Could we leave a note here about the money?" Ruth Rose asked.

"Good idea, Ruth Rose. I'll stick it up near my bait tanks."

The kids followed Ron into his bait shop, where he handed Ruth Rose a pencil and pad.

She thought for a minute, then wrote:

If you lost money on Squaw Island, call 555-9916.

"Shouldn't you say how much you found?" Josh asked.

Ruth Rose shook her head. "If I write the amount, anyone could call and claim it, even if they didn't lose it."

Ron tacked Ruth Rose's note to a small bulletin board. "Lots of people will see it here," he said.

"Thanks, Mr. P," Ruth Rose said. "I hope whoever lost the money sees the note."

Ron grinned. "Wish it was me!"

The kids laughed. They said goodbye and headed for Duck Walk Way.

"So what're you gonna do with the money?" Josh asked Ruth Rose. "I'll be glad to hold on to it for you!"

Ruth Rose shook her head. "Nope. I'm giving it to Officer Fallon. It'll be safe at the police station."

Josh scratched his arm. "Let's stop at Ellie's on the way. Maybe an ice cream cone will help me forget about this lousy poison ivy!"

The kids crossed the elementary school's wide lawn and hiked down Main Street. As they opened the door to Ellie's Diner, cool air washed over them.

After they ordered cones, Ruth Rose asked Ellie if she knew anyone who had lost money on Squaw Island.

"Someone with really huge feet!" Dink added.

Ellie shook her head. "Hon, I don't even know

anyone who goes out there. I hear it's covered with poison ivy!"

She noticed Josh scratching. "Looks like someone else is covered with the stuff!"

The kids thanked Ellie and left. They worked on their cones on the way to the police station.

"I can't believe we're gonna just give away a hundred bucks," Josh said.

"If I get a reward," Ruth Rose said, "I'll split it with you guys."

Josh grinned. "Now you're talking!"

They found Officer Fallon sitting at his desk. He was watching his computer screen and sipping a glass of lemonade.

"Howdy," he said as the kids trooped in. "What can I do for you?"

"Look at this!" Ruth Rose said. She placed the hundred-dollar bill on his desk.

Officer Fallon picked up the bill and examined it. "Where'd this come from?" he asked.

"Ruth Rose found it on Squaw Island," Josh told him. "We were out there having a picnic, and it was in the sand!"

"I'm trying to find out who lost it," Ruth Rose said. "Mr. Pinkowski let me put a note on his bulletin board. I left my phone number."

"This bill could've been lost a long time ago," Officer Fallon said. "Not many folks go to Squaw Island."

He grinned at Ruth Rose. "If no one claims it, the money is yours to keep."

"Really?" Ruth Rose said. "Cool!"

隐形岛

Officer Fallon put the bill in an envelope and sealed it. He wrote the date and Ruth Rose's name on the outside.

"I'll put this in our safe," he said. "If it's still here in thirty days, I'll let you know."

The kids thanked Officer Fallon and left.

"Gee, Ruth Rose," Josh said as they waited for the light on Main Street. "Will you split the hundred three ways if you get to keep it?"

"I might," she said. "If you're extra nice to me!"

"I'm always nice to you!"

Dink whispered something in Ruth Rose's ear.

"Okay, prove you're nice," she told Josh. "Come over tomorrow and mow my lawn!"

Josh laughed. "I have a better idea. Let's go back to the island and look for more money!"

"Josh, we already did, and there wasn't any," Dink said.

"But we never found where the footprints ended," Josh argued. "I'll bet if we do, we'll find buried treasure!"

"What about the poison ivy?" Ruth Rose reminded him.

Josh scratched his neck. "So what's a little poison ivy?" he said. "I'm going back to Squaw Island tomorrow, and I'm bringing a shovel!"

He grinned at his friends. "You coming with me? Or do I keep the treasure all to myself?"

Chapter 4

Dink yawned and looked out the kitchen window the next morning.

"Fog," he muttered. He finished his cereal and put the bowl in the sink.

Just then, the doorbell rang. It was Josh, standing on the porch holding a shovel. "You ready to go?" he asked.

"It's so foggy," Dink said, looking over Josh's shoulders. "I can hardly see across the street! We won't find the island, let alone a treasure."

"If there's more money out there, I'll find it," Josh said, scratching his ankle. "Let's get Ruth Rose."

"I'm already here!" Ruth Rose said, appearing out

of the fog.

When she saw Josh scratching, she said, "You better put something on that poison ivy, Joshua!"

"My mom said the same thing," Josh said. He scratched his arm. "She gave me money to buy some calamine lotion. Now let's get going!"

Balancing the shovel over one shoulder, Josh led his friends through Ruth Rose's backyard and across Meadow Road. The tall, dewy grass on the other side soaked their sneakers and legs.

Near the river, the fog was even thicker. It hung in tree branches like miniature clouds. The kids' faces and hair were wet.

"I can't even see the river," Dink muttered.

"It's right here," Josh said, splashing the water with his shovel.

"Yeah, but where's the island?" Ruth Rose asked.

The kids gazed out to where they thought Squaw Island should be. All they could see was more fog. One patch looked a little darker than the rest.

"That must be it," Josh said, stepping into the water. "Come on, guys, I can almost smell the money!"

"Like a hound dog," Dink muttered.

The river was quiet. No birds sang. The kids' legs splashing through the water was the only sound.

Dink began to imagine some fog monster creeping toward him. It had slimy green tentacles and six-inch-long teeth!

Dink was glad when the water became shallower. Suddenly, his foot struck dry land. They were on Squaw Island again!

The kids stopped and looked around. Wisps of fog hung over everything. Dink could barely make out the mound of boulders in the center of the island. He remembered yesterday's sun on his back and shivered.

"This place is creepy in the fog," Ruth Rose said. "I hope the sun comes out soon!"

"Okay, Joshua," Dink said. "You got us out here. Now what?"

Josh dropped to his hands and knees. "Help me find the big footprints again," he said.

The kids quickly found the prints and followed them to the squat, vine-covered boulder.

"So where'd Bigfoot go from here?" Josh muttered.

"It looks like the guy walked right into this big rock," Dink said.

"Maybe he climbed over it," Ruth Rose said.

Josh poked his shovel into the poison ivy vines covering the boulder. The shovel clinked against stone. Josh tried another spot. This time the shovel went straight in.

"Hey, guys!" Josh said. "I think I found something!"

Using the shovel to keep the vines back, Josh peered into a dark space.

"There're two boulders here!" he said.

"And look," Ruth Rose said. "A little path goes right between them!"

The path was hidden, covered with poison ivy leaves and vines.

"He must have gone through there," Dink said.

"But it's all poison ivy!" Ruth Rose said.

"Wait a sec," Josh said. He chopped at the poison ivy with his shovel until he had cleared a passage. "Just be careful," he said.

Single file, the kids walked down the narrow path. Enormous boulders loomed over them on each side.

Soon they came to a small, sandy clearing in the middle of the rocks. The rocks were thick with poison ivy. The dew-covered leaves were dull green in the fog.

"I feel like I'm in some jungle!" Ruth Rose said.

"More prints!" Josh said, dropping down on his knees.

Dink got down next to Josh. "They look like they're from the same guy," Dink said. "But there are so many! And they walk all over each other."

"Now what, Josh?" Ruth Rose asked.

"Now we search for treasure," Josh said. "We'll take turns and dig all over this place!"

They began digging hole after hole. Ruth Rose found a rusty nail, but no treasure.

Soon the kids were sweaty and covered with sand. Josh started filling the holes back in so no one would step in them.

Dink flopped down against one of the boulders.

"WATCH OUT!" Ruth Rose yelled.

Dink jumped away from the rock. Something was sticking him through his shirt!

"Ouch! What's poking me?" he asked. He turned around so Josh and Ruth Rose could see his back. "Can you see anything?"

Josh grinned. "Just a hunk of poison ivy," he said.

"Stop grinning and get it off me!" Dink yelled.

"I'll get it," Ruth Rose said. She brushed at the twig with the shovel handle.

"Is it gone?" Dink asked, trying to see over his

shoulder.

"This is amazing!" Ruth Rose said. "Look, Josh!"

"I don't believe it," Josh said.

"What's amazing?" Dink cried. "What're you guys doing back there?" He was already feeling itchy.

"This poison ivy is fake!" Ruth Rose said.

"Huh?" Dink turned around. Ruth Rose handed him a green sprig. The leaves were plastic and the stem was made of brown wire.

"I don't get it," Dink said. "Why would anyone …"

"This is too weird," Josh said. He placed the shovel blade between the boulder and the fake poison ivy. Then he twisted the shovel and pried off a section of vines. It came away from the face of the boulder in a sheet and fell flat on the ground.

"The whole rock is covered with plastic poison ivy," Ruth Rose said. "Tied to a wooden frame!"

"Forget that," Josh said. "Look what was under this stuff!"

The "boulder" wasn't a boulder at all. The kids were staring at a large square cement slab.

Chapter 5

"What is it?" Dink and Ruth Rose asked at the same time.

"It looks like a cement refrigerator!" Josh said.

Ruth Rose laughed. "Gee, Josh, I wonder if there's food in it!"

"Very funny!" Josh climbed up on some smaller rocks and hoisted himself to the top of the slab.

"It's flat up here, too," he said. "This thing is a big cement box!"

"Is this front part a door?" Ruth Rose asked. She poked the flat slab with the shovel.

Dink ran his fingers along the sides. "I can't find

any hinges," he said. He tugged at it, but it didn't budge.

"Maybe there's a secret lock somewhere," Ruth Rose suggested. She began digging around the bottom of the slab. All she found was stones and poison ivy roots.

"Ouch!" Josh said, still on top. "There's something sharp up here!"

He poked his head over the top. "Climb up here, guys. I think I found the key to this thing!"

Dink and Ruth Rose scrambled up next to Josh.

"Look at this," Josh said. He pointed to a metal rod poking out of the cement.

"Try pulling on it," Dink suggested.

Josh grabbed the rod and yanked. "Doesn't come

out," he muttered.

"Does it wiggle back and forth?" Ruth Rose asked.

She put her foot against the rod and shoved. It still didn't budge.

"Well, it has to do something," Dink said.

He climbed down off the cement box, grabbed the shovel, and handed it up to Josh.

"Try hitting it with that," he said.

Josh held the shovel over his head, braced himself, and gave the rod a good smack.

Suddenly, they heard a scratchy noise, like fingernails on a chalkboard.

"Whoa, that did it!" Dink yelled, jumping back. "It's moving!"

The cement door swung open, revealing a damp, musty closet.

Dink took a step forward, then stopped. His jaw dropped.

"What's in there?" Josh asked, staring down at Dink.

Dink didn't answer.

"Dink?" Ruth Rose said. "What's going on?"

Dink gulped and tried to speak. "Muh-muh-muh …"

"What the heck is 'muh'?" Josh said. "Mud? Mummies? Muffins?"

Dink could barely breathe, let alone talk.

"Money!" he finally said.

Chapter 6

Josh and Ruth Rose scrambled down and stared into the opening.

Inside, it was like a vault. Metal shelves had been attached to the cement walls with thick bolts. And every shelf held money.

Stacks of green bills were piled one on top of another. Everywhere Dink looked, he saw wads and wads of money.

"There must be millions of dollars in here!" Josh said. He closed his eyes. "I think I'm gonna throw up."

"But whose money is it?" Ruth Rose asked. "Who put it here?"

Dink stepped inside the vault. On the bottom

shelves were cardboard boxes with HAPPY HEART DOG FOOD written on the sides.

"Dog food?" he said.

Josh and Ruth Rose crowded into the vault. Ruth Rose peeked into two of the boxes.

"More money," she said.

Suddenly, Dink looked back over his shoulder. "Shhh!" he whispered. "I think I heard something!"

The kids stood perfectly still and listened.

"There it is again!" Dink said.

A muffled squeaking sound came through the fog. Then there was silence, then another squeak.

Dink gulped, frozen to the spot. "It's coming

closer!" he whispered.

"M-maybe it's the p-pirate!" Josh said.

"It could be the guy with big feet!" said Ruth Rose. "Maybe this is his treasure!"

"Let's get out of here!" Dink said. "Help me close this thing!"

The kids swung the cement door shut. Josh grabbed his shovel while Dink and Ruth Rose lifted the plastic poison ivy back into place. Now the cement safe was hidden again.

Dink quickly led the way back through the boulders to the water.

On the narrow beach, they stood in the fog and listened.

Dink heard the squeaking sound again, then a soft thud, then silence.

Slowly, a small boat drifted out of the fog. A large, dark figure sat hunched in the stern. Dink didn't dare move or say anything. It looked as if the figure was staring at them!

After what seemed like a year, the figure began to row away. Dink heard the oars squeak as the boat vanished back into the fog.

"Wh-who was that?" Josh croaked.

"I don't know," Dink said.

"Whoever it was, let's get off this island!" Ruth Rose said.

The kids quietly stepped into the shallow water. Trying not to splash, they waded to shore. Dink kept watch for the boat and its silent passenger. But he couldn't see anything through the fog.

Behind them, Squaw Island became invisible once

more.

Ten minutes later, they flung open the door to Officer Fallon's office.

Officer Fallon looked up from his computer. "What's wrong, kids? You look like you've seen a ghost!"

He stared at their soggy sneakers. "And you're all wet!"

"We found more money," Ruth Rose said. "Millions of dollars!"

Officer Fallon raised one eyebrow.

"Really, we did!" Josh said.

"Okay, sit down and talk to me," Officer Fallon said, switching off his computer.

The kids perched on the edges of their chairs.

"We went back to the island," Dink explained, "and found a cement safe. It had stacks of money in it!"

They told Officer Fallon about the secret path, the

plastic poison ivy, and the hidden cement vault.

"Just before we left, we saw someone in a rowboat," Josh said. "I think he was coming to the island, but then he turned around and left!"

Officer Fallon sat up. "Did you get a good look at him?" he asked.

"It was too foggy," Dink said.

Officer Fallon frowned and nodded.

"Why would anyone keep money on Squaw Island?" Ruth Rose asked. "Why wouldn't they just keep it in a regular bank?"

Officer Fallon looked at Ruth Rose. "Because it's not real money," he said.

"It's not?" Ruth Rose asked. "What is it, then?"

"I guess there's no reason not to tell you," Officer Fallon said. "After you left yesterday, I remembered something I read a few weeks ago about counterfeit money. I took a closer look at the bill you found."

He pulled the envelope from his drawer and removed the hundred-dollar bill. "This is counterfeit, kids. And I'm guessing the money in your cement safe is counterfeit, too."

"Counterfeit?" Josh gasped. "You mean it's all fake?"

Officer Fallon smiled. "Sorry, Josh."

"But who put it there?" Dink asked.

"That's what we're trying to find out," Officer Fallon said.

He stood and walked the kids to the door. "Officer Keene and I will go out there for a look today. Starting now, we'll be keeping an eye on that island."

Officer Fallon opened his office door. "Off you go now. And promise me you'll stay away from that island. Counterfeiters can be dangerous!"

The kids thanked Officer Fallon and left. As they walked up Main Street, Dink thought about the mysterious figure he'd seen in the boat. Was it the counterfeiter? Had he seen the three of them standing on the beach?

Dink swallowed. Were he and Josh and Ruth Rose in danger?

Chapter 7

Josh scratched his knee, then his neck, then his left elbow.

"Guess I'd better buy some calamine lotion," he said.

"We're almost at the supermarket," Dink said. He glanced over his shoulder.

"What're you looking at?" Ruth Rose asked.

Dink shrugged. "Nothing, I guess. I just keep thinking about that creepy guy in the boat."

"Do you think he recognized us?" Josh asked. "I mean, if we couldn't see his face, maybe he couldn't see ours."

"I hope you're right," Dink said. "If the guy in the

boat was the counterfeiter, he could be anyone, even someone we know!"

"Oh, great, Dinkus," Josh said. "Now I'm going to have nightmares!"

The kids walked into the supermarket and headed for the pharmacy. Mrs. Hernandez looked up and smiled.

"Hi, kids, what do you need?" she asked.

Josh scratched his knee. "Do you have any calamine lotion?" he asked.

Mrs. Hernandez came out from behind her counter. She gave Josh a once-over.

"That's poison ivy, all right," she said. She took a pink bottle from a shelf and handed it to Josh. "That's my last bottle. Ron Pinkowski came in yesterday and bought up my other three."

Josh paid Mrs. Hernandez and thanked her. Then the kids left the store. They sat on a bench while Josh dabbed calamine lotion on his itchy spots.

"I wonder why Mr. P needs this stuff," Ruth Rose said. "Didn't he tell us he stays away from poison ivy?"

A to Z 神秘案件

"He wasn't scratching when we saw him yesterday," Dink said.

Suddenly, Josh jumped to his feet. "Oh, my gosh! It's him!"

Dink looked around. "Who's him?"

"Mr. Pinkowski!" Josh said. "He bought the calamine lotion because he's got poison ivy. And he's got poison ivy because he was on Squaw Island hiding his counterfeit money!"

Dink shook his head. "If Mr. P has poison ivy, he could've gotten it anywhere."

"Maybe he's hiding a printing press in one of his empty fish tanks!" Josh said.

隐形岛

"Josh, what are you talking about?" Ruth Rose asked.

"It's perfect!" Josh said. "He sells bait to fool people, but he's really getting rich making phony money!"

"That's crazy," Dink said. "Just because Mr. P bought calamine lotion doesn't mean he's a counterfeiter."

Josh screwed the bottle cap on and shoved the lotion into a pocket. "I'm not crazy!" he said. "He's tall, so he's probably got big feet, right?"

Ruth Rose opened her mouth, but Josh cut her off.

"And he lives right on the river," Josh went on. "He's got boats! He knows Squaw Island is the perfect place to stash money. It has to be him!"

Dink looked at Ruth Rose. "What do you think?" he asked her.

"It could have been Mr. Pinkowski in the boat," Ruth Rose said. "But he's our friend. I can't believe he's a counterfeiter!"

"I can't either," Dink said.

"Well, I can!" Josh said. He scratched his stomach. "Let's go back to the bait shop and see if he has poison ivy."

"But how will we know?" Ruth Rose asked.

Josh grinned. "He bought three bottles of calamine lotion," he reminded her. "He'll be pink!"

Dink laughed. "Okay, let's go back to the bait shop," he said. "You look for poison ivy. I want to see if Mr. P's feet are as big as those footprints!"

Chapter 8

"Well, you were right about one thing," Ruth Rose whispered to Josh. "Mr. Pinkowski does have big feet!"

"Yeah, but they still don't look as big as those footprints we saw," Dink whispered back.

The kids were hiding behind the bushes near Ron's Bait Shop. Ron was standing in his yard, rubbing a cloth over a small green rowboat.

"Look at that boat!" Josh said. "It could be the one we saw out at the island!"

"But I don't see any calamine lotion on him," Dink said. "And he's not scratching!"

Just then, a black car pulled into the driveway. Ron waved as a man in a dark suit stepped out of the car.

The man waved back, then leaned into the car and pulled out a box. On its side were written four words: HAPPY HEART DOG FOOD!

Josh gasped. "Do you see …"

"Shhh!" whispered Ruth Rose.

The kids watched as the man handed Ron the box. Ron turned and carried it into his shed.

When Ron came out, he handed the box back to the stranger. The man put it on the seat of his car, then took out a checkbook. Quickly, he scribbled out a check and handed it to Ron.

Finally, he climbed back in his car and drove away.

"Check out the license plate!" Ruth Rose said.

Dink read the plate. "B, E, N, T. BENT? What's that mean?" he asked.

"Who cares?" Josh said. "Mr. P just sold that guy a boxful of counterfeit money! Let's go tell Officer Fallon!"

"Josh, that box could have been full of dog food," Dink said.

"Dinkus, think!" Josh said. "Someone hid fake money in those same dog food boxes on Squaw Island. I say one of those two guys is the counterfeiter!"

"Josh could be right," Ruth Rose pointed out. "But before we go see Officer Fallon, maybe we can find out who that other man is."

"How?" Dink asked.

"Let's ask at the gas station," Ruth Rose said. "Mr. Holly might know who drives a black car with BENT on the license plate."

When the kids reached the gas station, Mr. Holly was nowhere in sight.

Then Dink heard someone whistling. The tune was coming from under a banged-up red pickup truck.

"Mr. Holly?" Dink said. "Is that you?"

A round, grease-smudged face popped out from under the truck.

"Howdy," Mr. Holly said, grinning at the kids. "You got car trouble?"

"Sort of," Ruth Rose said. "Do you know who owns a car with BENT on the license plate?"

Mr. Holly stood up and wiped his hands on a rag. "Why, is the car bent?" he said, winking at Dink.

Dink laughed. "No, but we need to find the driver," he said.

"I found some money," Ruth Rose said. "We think it might be his."

"Sounds like those new folks," Mr. Holly said, "Mr. and Mrs. Warden Bent. Few weeks ago, they rented a small house on Fox Lane. I put a set of spark plugs in that snazzy Lincoln of theirs."

"Fox Lane!" Dink said, giving Josh a look. "That's over by the river!"

"Right-o," Mr. Holly said. "Nice view of the water. Now if you'll excuse me, this old truck needs my help!"

The kids thanked Mr. Holly and left the gas station.

"We know who the guy is now," Dink said, "but we still can't prove he or Mr. P is a counterfeiter."

"But the box—" Josh started to say.

"We don't know what was in it," Dink reminded him.

145

"Right," Ruth Rose said. "Why don't we go to Mr. Bent's house and wait for him to come home? Maybe we can get a peek at the box when he goes in his house."

"Okay, but let's be careful," Dink said. "I don't want to end up locked in that vault on Squaw Island!"

Chapter 9

The kids crossed Thistle Court and headed toward Fox Lane.

There were only three small houses on the narrow lane. The last one was a cottage nearly hidden in trees and thick bushes. Somewhere, a bird let out a single chirp.

Josh nudged Dink. "The car!" he whispered, pointing.

The same black car was parked under a tree. The license plate said BENT.

The kids snuck up to the car. All three peered through a rear window.

There was no Happy Heart Dog Food box on the

car's seats or floor.

"He must've taken it into the house," Dink said, crouching down next to Josh and Ruth Rose.

"Now what do we do?" Josh asked.

"We could try getting inside the house," Ruth Rose said.

Josh looked at her. "How?"

"What if we ring the bell and say we're selling Girl Scout cookies?"

Josh rolled his eyes. "Yeah, right, two boys selling Girl Scout cookies!"

"Okay, then I'll do it alone," Ruth Rose said.

"No way," Dink said. "No one's going into that house. If the Bents are the counterfeiters, they're dangerous!"

"So what do we do?" Josh asked. "I sure could use a sandwich!"

Suddenly, the front door opened. A short-legged hound dog with floppy ears waddled out onto the porch. The dog was brown and white, with big, sad eyes.

"Stay near the house, Shorty," a voice said.

"Uh-oh," Josh whispered.

"Let's get out of here before he smells us!" Ruth Rose said.

The kids melted into the thick shrubbery growing wild on both sides of the cottage. They crept toward the backyard, trying to be as quiet as possible.

"Look," Dink said, pointing to a small garage at the very back of the property. Except for the door, the garage was surrounded by bushes. "We can hide there!"

Just then, the dog let out a howl.

Ruth Rose looked over her shoulder. "Oh, no! He's after us!"

The kids sprinted behind the garage. Dink found a low window.

"In here!" he said, shoving the window sash up.

The dog came loping around the corner with its nose to the ground.

"Nice doggie," Josh whispered.

The hound looked at Josh and let out another howl.

"Quick, inside!" Dink said. He dove through the

open window.

Josh and Ruth Rose piled into the garage on top of Dink. Outside, the dog started barking. Dink saw its black snout and eyes peeking over the sill. He shoved Josh off him and closed the window.

The dog was still barking. It scratched at the window with its big feet.

"We have to hide!" Dink said. "The Bents are bound to hear all that noise!"

The kids quickly looked around. Against one wall, a workbench was piled with junk. Dink noticed a tarp-covered mound opposite the bench.

隐形岛

Josh and Ruth Rose dove under the bench. Dink headed for the tarp. He lifted one edge, crawled underneath, and let the tarp drop over his back.

It was dark under the tarp. Dink couldn't see a thing. He found himself sprawled on top of several hard boxes with sharp edges.

Suddenly, the dog stopped barking. Dink thought he heard a human voice.

He lifted a corner of the tarp and peeked toward the window. Through the dirty glass, Dink saw a woman's legs. She bent down, picked up the dog, and carried him out of sight.

Barely breathing, Dink waited until he felt sure the woman wasn't coming back. Then he crawled out from under the tarp. On the other side of the garage, Josh and Ruth Rose came out from under the bench.

"That was close!" Ruth Rose said.

Dink looked around. They were standing on a cement floor. The air was cool and dry. In one corner stood gardening tools and a few fishing poles.

Then Dink spotted something. "Look!" he said.

On top of the workbench sat a Happy Heart Dog Food box.

"Maybe it's the one Mr. Bent had in his car!" Dink said. He yanked open the box flaps. Inside, he found only a paint can with green smears on its sides.

Dink thought for a minute. "Guys, remember that boat Mr. P was working on? It was green, right?"

He held up the paint can. "Maybe the boat belongs to Mr. Bent, and Ron painted it for him. This could be the leftover paint."

"Then the check Mr. Bent gave him was to pay for the paint job!" Ruth Rose said.

She reached into the box and pulled out a wadded ball of paper. She flattened it on the workbench.

"It's a receipt from the pharmacy," Ruth Rose said. "For three bottles of calamine lotion!"

Dink stared at the receipt. It was from a credit card. Neatly printed on the bottom of the piece of paper was the name Ronald W. Pinkowski.

"Hey, guys, check this out!"

Josh had been poking around the other side of the garage. Hanging on wall pegs were two pairs of long green wading boots.

Josh unhooked one pair and took it down. "Look at the size of this foot!" he said.

Dink walked over for a closer look. "These must be what made those big footprints!" he said.

Ruth Rose examined the bottom of one of the boots. Wedged into the treads were tiny pebbles and sand.

The kids stared at each other.

"Now what do we do?" Josh asked.

"Now we go tell Officer Fallon what we found," Dink said.

He tiptoed over to the garage door and peeked

through a crack.

"Uh-oh," Dink said. "We're in trouble, guys. Mrs. Bent just brought out some food. She's lighting the grill!"

"Great," Josh muttered. "And I'm stuck in here, starving to death!"

He and Ruth Rose joined Dink at the crack.

"Look!" Ruth Rose said.

A tall man walked up to the grill. It was the

man they'd seen at Ron's Bait Shop. But now he was wearing shorts and a T-shirt.

His long arms and legs were blotched with calamine lotion.

Chapter 10

Ruth Rose let out a small gasp. "He's the one who got poison ivy on Squaw Island! The calamine lotion was for him!"

"But Mr. Pinkowski bought it," Josh said. "I still say they're in it together!"

Dink peeked through the garage door crack again. "Mr. Bent's reading a newspaper," he whispered. "Mrs. Bent's cooking hamburgers."

"Is the dog there?" Josh asked.

"Yep."

"If we try to leave, the dog will probably start barking again," Ruth Rose said.

"Those hamburgers smell so good!" Josh said. He

let out a little groan.

"Don't think about food," Dink said. "Think about a way to get us out of here!"

"Okay, I will!" Josh said. He shoved Dink aside and put an eye to the crack. "I have a plan," he said after a minute.

"Tell us!" Ruth Rose said.

Josh grinned. "Let's invite the Bents into the garage!"

Ruth Rose shook her head. "The poison ivy has finally gotten to his brain," she said to Dink.

"No, listen," Josh said. "We'll make a lot of noise. The Bents and poochie will hear it. They'll come flying in here to find out what's going on and—"

"And catch us in their garage!" Dink interrupted.

Josh smiled devilishly. "Nope, because we'll be hopping out the window. They'll never see us!"

Dink nodded thoughtfully. "It could work," he said. "But I think we need to figure out a way to keep them in here long enough for us to get away."

"I have an idea!" Ruth Rose walked over to the workbench. "There must be something to write with," she muttered.

"What're you gonna write?" Josh asked.

"Aha!" Ruth Rose pulled a hunk of carpenter's chalk out of a toolbox.

She kneeled on the floor and printed in large letters:

I know about your counterfeit money. Let's talk or I go to the cops. Meet me on Squaw Island in an hour.

"Oh, my gosh!" Josh yelped.

"But what if they just go out to the island, take the money, and leave town?" Dink asked.

"Exactly! When they do, Officer Fallon will be waiting for them!" Ruth Rose said.

Josh found a hammer in the toolbox. "Find me something to bang on," he told Dink. "Then get ready to move!"

"I'll keep an eye outside!" Ruth Rose said, heading for the garage door.

Dink glanced around the garage, then walked over to the tarp he'd hidden under. He yanked the tarp away and let out a low whistle. "Guys, look!"

Josh and Ruth Rose hurried over. Dink had uncovered four Happy Heart Dog Food boxes.

Dink tore open one flap and peeked inside.

"Just cans of dog food," he said.

"He must use the empty boxes to carry the fake money," said Ruth Rose.

Josh spotted an empty pail. "I bet I can get their attention with this!" he said.

Dink opened the window. Ruth Rose came over to stand beside him.

"Okay, Josh," Dink said. "Do it!"

Josh took a deep breath, then started pounding the bottom of the pail with the hammer.

The noise boomed through the garage like thunder.

"Now!" Josh said. He dropped the hammer and pail and bolted for the window.

The kids hopped out and crouched in the weeds.

A few seconds later, they heard the garage door creak open and Mr. Bent say, "Stay, Shorty!"

Then Dink heard Mrs. Bent say, "Warden,

someone's been in here. Something's written on the floor!"

That was all the kids needed to hear. They raced toward the trees on the other side of the house. In two minutes, they had crossed the high school playing field and were heading down Main Street.

"I sure hope Officer Fallon is in," Dink said, out of breath.

He was. The kids burst through his door with red faces.

Officer Fallon looked up. "What are you— "

"We found the counterfeiter!" all three kids yelled.

Chapter 11

Interrupting each other, the kids told Officer Fallon about the Bents.

Even before Officer Fallon heard about the Happy Heart Dog Food boxes, he was shouting orders into his telephone.

"Don't go back to Fox Lane!" were his last words before he leaped for the door and disappeared.

"Now what?" Dink asked.

"Why should we be left out?" Ruth Rose asked. "Let's go watch!"

"Go where?" Josh asked. "He said to stay away—"

"Not Fox Lane," Dink interrupted. "The action is gonna be on Squaw Island!"

Minutes later, they were catching their breath next to Officer Fallon's cruiser on River Road. The fog had lifted and they had a better view of Squaw Island.

Dink peered across the river but saw only sand and rocks.

Out of breath, Josh sank to the ground. "I think I'm having a heart attack!" he moaned.

"Do you think Officer Fallon is out there?" Ruth Rose asked, squinting. "I don't see anyone."

The kids sat in the shade of the cruiser and watched the island.

Suddenly, Josh jumped to his feet. "There they are!" he shouted.

Three figures had come around the island's other side. It was too far away to tell who they were, but Dink thought he could see Officer Fallon's dark uniform.

Then a fourth person came into view. He was pulling a small flat-bottomed boat behind him.

"It's Officer Fallon and Officer Keene!" Dink said. "They've got the Bents!"

The kids watched the group come closer. The water was nearly up to Officer Fallon's knees. He led the Bents, who were handcuffed. Officer Keene waded behind, pulling the boat. It was green!

"Look what's in the boat!" Josh said. "It's piled with money and dog food boxes!"

Nobody spoke as Officer Fallon led the two counterfeiters to shore. The Bents were wearing their long wading boots. Their faces were angry as they stumbled up the riverbank.

Officer Keene pulled the boat ashore and loaded the counterfeit money into the trunk of the cruiser. Officer Fallon opened the rear door for the Bents, then locked it once they were inside.

"Good job," he said to the kids. He looked at Josh. "Are your folks home?"

"I don't know," Josh answered.

"Meet me at your house in an hour," Officer Fallon said. Then he and Officer Keene hitched up their wet pants and climbed into the cruiser.

The car sped away, leaving the air filled with dust and pine needles.

"Why does Officer Fallon want to talk to your mom and dad?" Dink asked, grinning. "Are you in trouble?"

"Gee, I wonder what jail food is like!" Ruth Rose said.

Dink patted Josh's belly. "I heard they feed the prisoners worm waffles for breakfast!"

"Tee-hee," Josh said. "You guys are so funny! He probably wants to give me a reward for catching the Bents."

"You didn't catch them," Ruth Rose said. "The three of us did!"

"But we all know I'm the brains in this group," Josh said, smiling.

They cut through a field to get to Josh's house. Josh yanked open the back door and yelled, "Anybody home?"

No one answered. "Let's eat," Josh said. "I'll make some sandwiches."

They sat in Josh's backyard with jelly sandwiches, paper cups, and a container of milk.

"I wonder where the Bents made the money," Dink said. "Do you suppose they have a printing machine in that house?"

Josh put his sandwich down. "What would it be like to make money whenever you wanted?"

Dink heard a car roll into Josh's driveway. A door slammed and Officer Fallon came around the house.

"Can you spare some of that milk?" he asked Josh.

"Sure!" Josh filled a cup and handed it to Officer Fallon.

He took a long sip, then looked at the kids. "The Bents are locked up, but they're not talking. When they do, I expect we'll find out they were just the middle guys. Whoever is printing all those hundreds is still out there somewhere."

"But why did the Bents hide the money on Squaw Island?" Josh asked.

"Easy to get to," Officer Fallon said. "With their boat at the bait shop, they could get out to the island in a few minutes."

"At first we thought they might be partners with Mr. Pinkowski," Dink said.

Officer Fallon nodded. "I can see why you thought so. I talked to Ron. He kept their boat in his yard. Then after Bent saw you kids on the island, he asked Ron to paint it. I guess he was afraid you would recognize it if you ever saw it again."

"Why did Mr. Pinkowski buy the calamine lotion?" Josh asked.

"Ron's a nice guy," Officer Fallon said. "I guess he noticed Bent was itching, so he bought him the lotion as a favor."

Officer Fallon glanced at Josh's barn. "Keep any animals in there?" he asked Josh.

"No," Josh said. "The twins and I want a pony, but Dad says they're too much work."

"How about a dog?" Officer Fallon said. "I just

happen to have a nice friendly basset hound who needs a good home."

Josh's eyes lit up. "Really?"

Officer Fallon smiled. "Maybe you two should get to know each other."

He whistled. Around the corner jogged Officer Keene, leading a short- legged dog with droopy ears.

"It's Shorty!" Ruth Rose said.

"You kids already know this pooch?" Officer Fallon said.

"He was at the Bents' house," Dink explained. "He almost gave away our hiding place!"

Officer Fallon stroked the dog's velvety ears. "Well, his owners are going to prison for a long time. He needs a new home."

Josh kneeled down and patted the dog's silky coat.

"Hey, doggie," he said. "You wanna live here?"

The dog gave Josh a lick with his long pink tongue, then plopped to the ground and rolled over.

"He likes me!" Josh said.

"I was counting on it," Officer Fallon said. He dropped the leash into Josh's hand and headed for his car. "Have your folks call me!" he said as he left.

"Thanks, Officer Fallon!" Josh called.

"What should we name him?" Josh asked after a minute.

"He already has a name," Ruth Rose reminded Josh. "Shorty."

Josh shook his head. "That's a terrible name. If you were short, would you want to be called Shorty?"

"Josh is right," Dink said. "We can come up with a better name than that."

But when Josh's parents came home an hour later, the kids still hadn't picked a name.

隐形岛

When Josh finally got permission to keep the dog, he still had no name.

Later that night, Dink, Josh, and Ruth Rose drifted off to sleep in their bedrooms.

The short-legged dog with droopy ears snored at the end of Josh's bed.

But he still had no name.

Text copyright © 1999 by Ron Roy
Illustrations copyright © 1999 by John Steven Gurney
All rights reserved under International and Pan-American Copyright Conventions.
Published in the United States by Random House, Inc., New York, and simultaneously
in Canada by Random House of Canada Limited, Toronto.

本书中英双语版由中南博集天卷文化传媒有限公司与企鹅兰登（北京）文化发展有限公司合作出版。

"企鹅"及其相关标识是企鹅兰登已经注册或尚未注册的商标。
未经允许，不得擅用。
封底凡无企鹅防伪标识者均属未经授权之非法版本。

©中南博集天卷文化传媒有限公司。本书版权受法律保护。未经权利人许可，任何人不得以任何方式使用本书包括正文、插图、封面、版式等任何部分内容，违者将受到法律制裁。

著作权合同登记号：字18-2023-258

图书在版编目（CIP）数据

隐形岛：汉英对照 /（美）罗恩·罗伊著；（美）约翰·史蒂文·格尼绘；高琼译. -- 长沙：湖南少年儿童出版社，2024.10. --（A to Z 神秘案件）.
ISBN 978-7-5562-7817-6

Ⅰ．H319.4

中国国家版本馆CIP数据核字第2024QK9595号

A TO Z SHENMI ANJIAN YINXING DAO

A to Z 神秘案件 隐形岛

[美] 罗恩·罗伊 著　[美] 约翰·史蒂文·格尼 绘　高琼 译

责任编辑：唐　凌　李　炜　　　　策划出品：李　炜　张苗苗　文赛峰
策划编辑：文赛峰　　　　　　　　特约编辑：杜天梦
营销编辑：付　佳　杨　朔　周晓茜　封面设计：霍雨佳
版权支持：王媛媛　　　　　　　　版式设计：马睿君
插图上色：河北传图文化　　　　　内文排版：马睿君

出 版 人：刘星保
出　　版：湖南少年儿童出版社
地　　址：湖南省长沙市晚报大道89号
邮　　编：410016
电　　话：0731-82196320
常年法律顾问：湖南崇民律师事务所　柳成柱律师
经　　销：新华书店
开　　本：875 mm × 1230 mm　1/32　　印　刷：三河市中晟雅豪印务有限公司
字　　数：96千字　　　　　　　　　　　　印　张：5.375
版　　次：2024年10月第1版　　　　　　　印　次：2024年10月第1次印刷
书　　号：ISBN 978-7-5562-7817-6　　　　定　价：280.00元（全10册）

若有质量问题，请致电质量监督电话：010-59096394　团购电话：010-59320018